LIVERPOOL

IT ALL CAME TUMBLING DOWN

Revised and Updated

A photographic survey and commentary on
Liverpool through the eyes and lens
of Freddy O'Connor

Cover picture view of South Castle Street/South John Street area L1 (1949)

This book is dedicated to my wonderful wife, Jean, who I tragically lost in April 2004, also to my dad, who I also tragically lost five months earlier.

I would like to thank the following members of my family for helping with this publication, brothers Frank, Ray and Peter, and Sister, Ann, My sons, Paul and Stephen, and daughter Helen.

The origional book *Liverpool It All Came Tumbling Down* was first published 1986. It covered the "Inner City Area" to Bootle in the North, Edge Hill to the East, and Dingle in the South.

All have been reproduced in this publication, and following the same route, the "updated" sections with many photographs never before published. "1986" indicates the original text and photographs and "updated" the previously unseen photographs plus new text together with selected views of Liverpool past.

All street names printed in **bold** represent the updated version.

NB: PH in this book refers to Public House.

PLEASE NOTE

Page 180 under 'South of the City Centre' should read '(1986)'

First Published 2013 by Countyvise Ltd
14 Appin Road, Birkenhead, CH41 9HH

Copyright © 2013 Freddy O'Connor

The right of Freddy O'Connor to be identified as the author of this work has been asserted by him in accordance with the Copyright, Design and Patents Act 1988.

British Library Cataloguing in Publication Data.
A catalogue record for this book is available from the British Library.

ISBN 978 1 906823 70 2

Foreword by Frankie Connor

Brothers in Arms (1986)

Frankie (left) and Freddy pictured in 1987, shortly after the first book's publication. The same year Frankie wrote and recorded his song 'Liverpool: It All Came Tumbling Down', first on vinyl, then the track featured on the C.D. 'Cavern Days' from the 'Class of '64' in 1992.

This book you are now reading began its life (unknowingly) over 50 years ago. 1961 was the year my younger brother Freddy first pointed his old Box Brownie camera at a subject so close to his heart: 'the streets of Liverpool'. He was just 13 years old.

Fast forward to 1983, when I called to his home in Anfield (where he still lives), for our usual walk through Stanley Park to Goodison Park and the football match. This particular day Freddy showed me several scrapbook albums containing all his photographs, laid out in order of date, district, year etc. A light went on in my head as I realised that this unique collection could possibly be turned into a local history book.

In 1984, with the help of Freddy's wonderful, late wife Jean, we tried every avenue to find a publisher. From Glasgow to Belfast, I wrote to companies, large and small; their reaction was strikingly similar: 'There won't be that much interest in old Liverpool streets'. We decided eventually to try and self-publish. So, I acquired some knee pads, arranged a bank loan and began working with a local company, Printfine Ltd. The book became a reality in January 1986 and I'm delighted to say, was a tremendous local success.

It is now 2013, and we felt that the time was right to re-print the book as many were sent to ex-pats living abroad and those copies may now be lost or others damaged. This larger, more comprehensive version contains the original pictures and text with the addition of many more unseen photographs: every single one a memory to somebody.

My brother and I come from a very close-knit family in the Scotland Road area and there is nobody more proud of 'our kid' than me, for having the 'foresight' (hindsight we all possess!!), coupled with his love for his city to capture the very streets and houses that so many of us came from. This may sound like a cliché in today's cynical climate, but many of these houses with their gleaming doorsteps and sparkling brass really were a source of pride to the families within.

Liverpool is a city forever moving forward, thriving and prospering on a worldwide scale and long may that continue for our children's children and beyond. Now, let this book take you back to another place in time. I hope the photographs and text will inform, surprise, perhaps provoke discussion, make you smile and possibly shed a tear as we remember a bygone era in Liverpool: 'The greatest city in the world'.

Freddy and I wish you a safe and memorable journey.

Contents

Preface (1986)

Time flies is an old saying, and it's certainly true, it's now just over a quarter of a century since my first publication: *Liverpool It All Came Tumbling Down.*

It was a collection of photographs taken by myself, and my brother Ray from the early 1960s, and even as late as the early 1980s. I hadn't even contemplated writing a book. However, with having so many photographs, mainly ordinary streets that were about to be demolished, or in the process of demolition, together with my other brother, Frank, we decided to gradually compile them into a book during the 1980s.

This was completed in 1986, and together with Frank, we began the task of getting it published, and that was by no means easy, in fact it became a mammoth task. "Rubbish" "no chance" "waste of time" and "that will never sell" were some of the better comments made to us by various publishers!

Of course not everyone came from the areas featured, therefore little interest to such people, and I can sum up the apathy by a grand old lady, when the book was finally published. For a short spell we had a "cart" in the Albert Dock to sell the book, and one day this elderly lady was glancing through the book when she remarked rather angrily "this isn't the proper Liverpool, just a load of old derelict houses".

I enquired where she was from, and she replied, "Mossley Hill, and it's not even mentioned". "Actually" I said, "it's on page nine, although only mentioned, not featured". I then went on to explain that the houses and streets were once homes and communities that were about to be wiped out in the inner City districts, hence the book's title, and that people who once lived in them were delighted to see their old stomping ground in print, when I'd often hear the phrases "I never thought I'd see that street again" or "I wish I'd have taken a photo of our street etc" numerous times.

When the penny dropped, like the majority of people at the cart, she then recalled her early days in rural Mossley Hill, and how it had changed over the years, recalling some wonderful stories of times gone by, exactly the same as people who lived in the streets featured, albeit completely different circumstances, the nostalgic stories, be it in rural Liverpool, or the inner City would come flooding back when old memories are reignited, and that was why the book became so popular.

Since compiling "Tumbling Down" I had "Liverpool Our City Our Heritage" published in 1990, then four volumes of "A Pub On Every Corner" in 1995, 1997, 1998, and 2001.

So into the second decade of the 21st century, and I've compiled "Tumbling Down, Revised and Up-Dated" the theme being similar to the first publication, former homes, streets and places throughout the inner City districts that are mainly demolished. Besides my own photographs, I have used some from various sources as acknowledged, many are within living memory, with others beyond living memory.

Liverpool's Development
(1986)

The development of any city's housing in terms of its styles and locations is inextricably wrapped up with its growth economically. Liverpool might well be described as a late developer. Although it was as early as 1207 that a Charter was issued by King John granting Liverpool the status of a borough, it was not until the seventeenth century that Liverpool's expansion began. Nonetheless part of the street system in the city centre dates back to the early thirteenth century. Chapel Street is one of the earliest streets named after a chapel, St Mary Del quay, which is thought to have been built in the thirteenth century. Nothing remains of the chapel but a similar site is now occupied by the parish church of Our Lady and St Nicholas known for centuries as the 'sailors church', for the Mersey originally flowed right past at the bottom of Chapel Street.

Other original streets are Dale Street, Tithebarn Street, High Street, Castle Street, Water Street and Old Hall Street and it was this area that first expanded as the importance of Liverpool as a port grew. The first dock, the Old Dock was built at Canning Place in 1715 and subsequent dock building during the eighteenth century included Canning Dock, Salthouse Dock and Georges Dock. The latter, opened in 1771 and enlarged in 1825, covered the area at the Pier Head between James Street and Chapel Street and so these old streets were right at the heart of the new dock system.

During the course of the 18th century the number of ships using the port, rose from 102 to 4,746, a dramatic rise by any standards. In the early and mid-eighteenth century Water Street was the fashionable home for the wealthiest of Liverpool's merchants but by the end of the eighteenth century these narrow streets were packed with traders, working from their shops and houses, and a growing number of warehouses. The wealthy began their flight from the centre, first to the Duke Street, Rodney Street and Canning Street area and then onto Upper Parliament Street. They also moved out into some of the outlying villages such as Kirkdale, Everton and Wavertree.

In the city centre land values soared and the area became the purely commercial centre it is today. Magnificent buildings were erected by businessmen to reflect their success and prestige. This culminated in the construction of the Pier Head group of offices. These were built between 1907 and the First World War on land reclaimed by the filling of Georges Dock. Incidentally the accurate name for this area is still Georges Pier Head named after the dock and a stone pier which projected into the Mersey at this point. There is still a small part called George's dock Gate where Chapel Street meets the dock road. The riverside of the dock road is called Goree as it runs past the Pier Head. This strange name derives from a bare rock off Cape Verde Island where slaves were gathered awaiting shipment to the plantations of the West Indies. The massive arcaded Goree Warehouses were built here in 1793 only to be destroyed by a fire, said to have lasted 3 months, in 1802. The warehouses were rebuilt but then destroyed during the blitz in 1941. Many fortunes were made in Liverpool through the slave trade and this appalling trade provided the foundations for many shipping lines. Few slaves would ever had reached the port though the *Liverpool Advertiser* of 1766 carried a notice for a sale of 11 Negro slaves to be held at the Exchange Coffee House in Water Street.

Liverpool City Centre, circa 1500. Showing the original Street Names.

6

Living in Liverpool
(1986)

It should not be thought that all was sweetness and light in the centre of early Liverpool. At the beginning of the seventeenth century Liverpool's population is estimated to have been roughly 2000. By 1700 it was only 6,000 but by 1801 it had grown to 80,000. Incredibly, in 1831 the figure had soared to 205,000. This population explosion was further boosted in the early and mid-nineteenth century by the huge influx of immigrants fleeing from famine conditions in Ireland. Inevitably all of this meant many people living in appalling conditions of squalor and disease.

Cellars provided homes for many. An investigation in 1790 revealed that in the city centre 2000 cellars were occupied by nearly 7000 people who lived in dark damp rooms with little or no sanitary provisions. The streets off Castle Street and Old Hall Street at what was then the northern end of the city, and around Park Lane in the south were infested with these atrocious cellars. It was no doubt the close proximity of the wealthy to such poverty that persuaded the rich to begin their exodus out of the city centre.

During this period and the early 1800s the other main form of slum dwelling, the courts, became well established. A court was the central yard, generally about 25 feet long and 10 feet wide, around which was constructed 2, 3 or 4 storey blocks of rooms on all sides. An average sized court generally housed 20 to 30 families. The front might well appear as a fairly ordinary terrace but once one entered the door or alley into the central court the poor conditions became only too obvious. The small windows received little light as the blocks were either very close together or might well be overshadowed by a high warehouse occupying one side of the court. One toilet and one tap in the central yard would probably be the only sanitary provisions, and in the early courts built before 1830, there would be no provision whatsoever and the occupants would have had to rely on cesspits. Hardly surprising that epidemics of diseases such as cholera, typhoid and smallpox were commonplace.

The areas containing such slums were soon no longer only found within the city centre where incidentally some streets such as Temple Court and Union Court still bear names reflecting their sordid past. The courts soon spread into the Vauxhall Road and Scotland Road areas in the north and Park Lane, St James Street and the Dingle area in the south. By 1841 a census showed that 56,000 people lived in these courts and a further 20,000 occupied cellars.

Many occupants were waiting to gain a passage on a ship to America and were only temporary residents. Liverpool was the main embarkation port to America for all of Europe and hundreds of thousands passed through the city over the decades. However, thousands, often those in poor health and with no money, were forced to remain here. They were the most vulnerable to the filthy conditions. In 1849 one of the many outbreaks of cholera killed over 5,000 people.

It is worth mentioning here that alcohol was another major social problem at this time. In the early 1800s there were no licensing laws and it has been estimated that one dwelling house in seven sold beer.

By the 1840s the gin palaces had appeared and there were over 2,000 licensed houses in Liverpool selling cheap drink to the working classes. Later in the century pubs became grander, more respectable and were accepted as part of the wider community.

Licensing hours, forcing them to close at midnight, were introduced in the 1870s and children were prohibited in 1901. Nonetheless it is hardly surprising that for many a skinful of cheap drink was the obvious escape from their terrible living conditions.

As the slums pushed out over a wider and wider area the wealthy middle classes fled before them. With the development of the early railways, travelling became less of a problem and many moved as far out as Mossley Hill, Aigburth and even distant Crosby in the north. Finally the terrible conditions were too disgraceful for the authorities to ignore any longer. In 1846 the Sanitary Act was passed in an attempt to improve housing conditions and Dr Duncan, the country's first Medical Officer of Health, was appointed.

From the mid-nineteenth century working class housing consisted mainly of terraces built particularly in then almost rural areas such as Everton and Kirkdale. Such houses showed a considerable improvement over the insanitary courts but were still totally unacceptable by today's standards. Some terraces (such as in Arley Street off Vauxhall Road) were little more than front doors opening into single rooms with a central door providing access to the rooms above.

From about the 1840s many streets of terraced housing were built with the backs of houses in two parallel streets being barely separated, either by a very narrow alley or a wall between two tiny back yards. These houses frequently had no windows at the back so that light could only enter at the front though this was not always as grim as it sounds as there was often only one room per floor. In 1864 an amendment was passed to the earlier Sanitary Act to try to improve matters further. 18,000 dwellings (still including 3,000 courts) were declared insanitary and the Act empowered the authorities to demolish them. Progress was slow and it took until 1914 for the city to have cleared 10,000, though private enterprise was responsible for some demolition too. About 400 courts were still standing at the outbreak of World War I. In 1869 the beginning of a revolution in house building occurred with the construction of the country's first municipal housing, St Martin's Cottages in Silvester Street. Although progress was slow here too, with the next major project not undertaken until 1880s when Victoria Square off Scotland Road was built, living conditions improved greatly towards the end of the century. The terraced houses of the late 1800s were usually two-up two-down with backyards and wider passages at the rear. The streets were wider and thus more light reached inside the rooms, probably all of which would by now have had windows. Housing of this type was built quite long distances from the centre of Liverpool spread in a huge fan shape from the centre. Garston, Wavertree and Walton, for example had, and still have, large amounts of housing from this period.

The Recent Past
(1986)

The development of housing in Liverpool during the twentieth century is the personal experience of many of us. The early landing houses have all gone but municipal tenements from the 20s, 30s and 40s are in varying states. Some have been cleared; a few have been renovated and given improved amenities and some of the later ones are still occupied though in desperate need of action. Unfortunately the last 30 years have done little to encourage our faith in local housing policy. The planners in their enthusiasm to improve upon the insanitary conditions, in which thousands were living, chose the indiscriminate use of the bulldozer rather than renovation. Not only were many fine buildings lost but whole communities were shattered. Families and friends were split up removing the network of support and help that existed for all. Worse, the new housing to which people were moved often created more problems for their occupants than the lack of an inside toilet had previously done. The two most unpleasant forms of rehousing from the 1950s have been high rise flats and new estates or towns built miles away from the centre. It is now universally acknowledged that high-rise housing was a mistake and many blocks, some less than 20 years old, have been demolished – partly in some cases because the quality of construction and design was so poor. Of the new estates Kirkby is the most famous post war

example, though isolated estates such as Speke built in the late 1930s were forerunners of this trend. The concept was that people should be rehoused outside the city in relatively rural surroundings. In fact, the residents of Kirkby regarded themselves as having been dumped in a field off the East Lancashire Road. Kirkby's facilities for shopping and entertainments were inadequate and buses into the city were infrequent, expensive and took a long time. Gone was the corner shop, the choice of pubs, the sense of community and, as the nearby industrial estate declined, gone was the chance of local work.

Lessons might have been learnt from experiences at Speke before Kirkby was ever built, for many of the problems were identical. However, the planners did not learn and it has taken a very long time for the mistakes made at Kirkby to be recognised. Many were repeated at Cantril Farm and Netherley; at Cantril Farm the planners forgot or thought unnecessary pavements on the estate leaving residents to walk on rough ground or share the roads with the traffic.

It seems that finally attitudes are changing. The emphasis now is on building low density estates much closer to the centre and, at last, renovation has been perceived as a cheaper and more satisfactory alternative to new building. It is tragic that so little is now left to renovate.

Liverpool and Tourism
(1986)

It is not only in housing policy that some terrible blunders have been made. Tourism is now widely regarded as one of the main industries for the city's future but we have already destroyed some of our potential tourist attractions.

Many examples of this short sightedness spring to mind. The Overhead Railway, or Docker's Umbrella as it was affectionately nicknamed, ran the length of the docks from Dingle to Seaforth. It was opened in 1893 as the first elevated, electrically operated railway in the world. The 'El' in New York was based on Liverpool's Overhead. When dock traffic declined in the 1950s the railway was closed and dismantled but how marvellous it would be now if some stretches at least had been preserved. The dock estate and dock road area has also lost many fine buildings though at least the finest, The Albert Dock, is being renovated.

The Beatles must be considered the most important tourist attraction of Liverpool today. The history of Beatles' success is known the fans the world over. Guided tours are now conducted around the city showing people where they lived and where Penny Lane can be found. There is one massive gap in this tour – The Cavern Club. I must admit to feeling personally very strongly about the demolition of the Cavern. As a teenager I regularly went there and in February 1966 I attended the closing night when, my brother Frank's group called 'The Hideaways' who played there a record number of times, were the last to appear. The Cavern re-opened 6 months later with 'The Hideaways' playing again and the event was thought important enough to attract celebrities such as Sir Harold Wilson, Ken Dodd, Jimmy Saville and Bessie Braddock MP. But the halcyon days were over, the now licensed club never recaptured its magic for me. Nonetheless when a foreign tourist gets into my taxi and asks for Mathew Street I can anticipate the look of disgust and disappointment on their face when I explain the Cavern Club was demolished. The new Cavern Walks shopping complex is fine but it is not what a Japanese fan has come to Liverpool to see. Once again the City has realised too late the error of its ways. Numerous magnificent pubs; the old heart of the city with its squares; many fine houses – the list is endless – have all been demolished with no thought of either the importance of the past or of the future.

Dock Road North and Bootle
(1986)

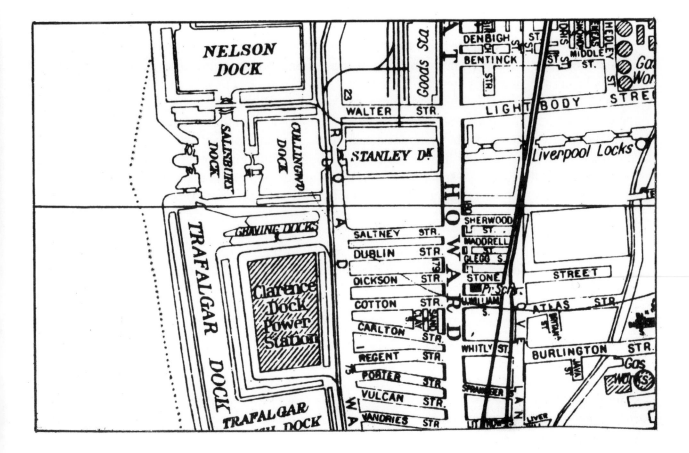

Although everyone in Liverpool habitually refers to 'the dock road', this name does not in fact officially exist. The dock road is merely the common term for a succession of separately named sections of road which run alongside the river to the north and to the south from the city centre. To the north the dock road begins as 'New Quay' at Princes Dock, then changes and becomes Bath Street. The name Bath Street comes from the 18th century sea water baths that were formerly sited here. The baths were demolished in 1817 when Princes Dock was being built. Princes Dock was opened on the coronation of King George IV in July 1821. It was at this period that Liverpool's commerce began to expand on an unprecedented scale. This was when many of the grand brick warehouses were built as the docks spread out from the old city centre transforming the former North Shore. The dock road was rightly famous for its incredible number of pubs, but only about 12 are still standing at the time of writing. In common with many parts of Britain, precise navigation of the dock road could be achieved via the names, both famous and infamous, of these pubs. One road, Vandries Street, (see page 13) was even named after a Dutchman who ran an ancient hostelry on the old North Shore.

Further north, the 'dock road' becomes Regent Road as far as Gladstone Dock. Not so long ago this long thoroughfare was bustling with activity but it is now quiet as the docks have gone into decline. The decline of shipping into the Port of Liverpool can be compared to the severing of a main artery. Jobs directly and indirectly linked with the sea were once the lifeblood of the City.

Even as late as the 1950s dockers alone numbered approximately 20,000 compared to under 3,000 now. The majority of families in the old parts of Liverpool had menfolk working in some capacity at the docks. Going away to sea was routine occupation for thousands of scousers, and I myself joined the Merchant Navy at the age of 16. Within two decades of my going away to sea, the job of the seaman was almost as extinct as the great liners that once frequented the port. Containerisation and other new technologies are reducing the size of ships' crews and there has been a decline in the overall volume of traffic too. The oil fired ships that I sailed on were a great improvement on their predecessors, the steam ships, upon which an entire culture and way of life was based. Working in the bowels of those steam powered infernos were the firemen and coal trimmers, many of them from Liverpool, such as my Uncle John Devitt from Scotland Road. My father served in the Royal Navy and together with many others who lived through the war years he told me about the work of these men. All agreed that if there was a harder task involved in any occupation they had not heard of it. The laborious job of the trimmers was to continually fetch coal for the firemen keeping the boilers fired, in temperatures of up to 130°. Steamships and the men who sailed in them are now just a memory in the annals of Liverpool's history, although their association with Liverpool will live on for some time to come.

The continued decline and demolition of Liverpool's waterfront is very evident along Regent Road into Bootle. However, it should not be forgotten that parts of the dockland area have been depopulated for many years, not so much because of the bulldozer and the recession but because of the heavy bomb damage during World War 2. Sandhills and Bootle still have much open space and occasionally more modern buildings as a result of wartime bombing.

The Great Howard Street area is an instructive sample of the changed and changing circumstances of the docklands. When St Augustine's Church (see photo page 17) was opened in 1849, Liverpool's already overcrowded slums were still being swelled by poor Irish immigrants. The church was opened in honour of three Benedictine monks who had died caring for the plague ridden poor who had inhabited this densely populated part of Dock Land. As time passed gradual improvements took place as the slums of the area disappeared, and by the First World War there were only about 3,000 left. The Second World War brought almost total devastation to the area and since then it has become mainly industrial with the residential population virtually nil. Throughout the bombing and demolition the church itself survived, but with depopulation of the area finally taking its toll, it closed in 1976.

This seven-storey warehouse on Bath Street was demolished in the late 1970s and the former dock road pub 'The International' is now used as a canteen.

Early nineteenth century warehouses on the Bath Street section of the dock road, demolished in the late 1970s.

Early nineteenth century warehouses being demolished in 1967 in Vandries Street, off the Waterloo Road section of the dock road.

The Regent Road section of the north dock road was once a thriving bustling thoroughfare before the dramatic post-war decline of commerce and shipping in Liverpool.

Saltney Street off Regent Road, with paved roadway and gas lights, still lit, in 1966. These 'landing' tenements, now demolished, were originally built in 1911 to replace the original infamous slum courts typical of the area.

Stanley Dock is the only dock on the landward side of the dock road. The warehouses were built in 1848 by the renowned dock engineer Jesse Hartley who designed the world famous Albert Dock complex south of the city centre.

This tobacco warehouse at Stanley Dock was built in 1900 and is reputed to be the largest warehouse in the world. The massive twelve storey structure of red and blue brick still stands.

The 'American Hotel', Regent Road, at the corner of Blackstone Street was one of the many famous dock road pubs. It was demolished in the 1980s.

Regent Road in Bootle was the location of this warehouse at Miller's bridge shown here during demolition in 1984. The crane in the background stands on the edge of Brocklebank Dock. In the background is the 'Mammoth' a steam driven floating structure which has worked throughout the docks since 1920. Together with Liverpool's only other floating crane – 'Samson' – it is to cease working later this year and more than likely demolished.

15

The small terraced houses in narrow Garden Lane near Park Street, also in Bootle, date from the 1860s and were cleared in 1969.

Derby Road, close to Bankhall.

The last block of the old property in Beacon Street at the junction with Boundary Street, was built in the 1830s. This notorious area was known as 'Sebastapol' from the 1850s.

St Augustines Church, built in 1849, in Great Howard Street.

Major changes have occurred in the north docks since my first publication in 1986. Now over two decades later, and of course a new millennium, like the south docks, the north docks are now mainly redundant from their original use, although the far north docks are still operating. The port has had "Freeport" status since the 1980s, and a major scheme, the Sandon Dock sewerage works was opened in 1991. That's part of a multi-million pound scheme, started some 40 years ago to clean up the Mersey, and still ongoing. Just a few decades ago the Mersey was amongst the dirtiest rivers in Europe, with the oxygen levels virtually nil, and the idea of fish in the river unthinkable, yet now the oxygen rate is some 60% and fish are becoming more and more plentiful, something not seen since before the industrial revolution, and of course enhancing the environment.

I featured a superb photograph of the Princes Dock in *Liverpool Our City, Our Heritage* together with a history of the dock estate, when that dock was the berth for the "Irish boats" with an Isle of Man boat at the landing stage, also a photograph of the derelict Princes half tide dock.

The 1990s was the start of a massive transformation of the Princes Dock, and the vicinity, now containing hotels and new office blocks, with further major schemes in the pipeline moving ever further north (see East Princes Dock, page 21). This is to be known as "Liverpool waters" a huge scheme that will transform the north docks completely from their original purpose, and one for the future of course, and so out of the scope of this book,

All photographs are accompanied by a postal district (when appropriate) and the L3 area is immediately north and east of the City Centre, yet it also covers the dock estate as far as the Canada Dock north, and Dingle point south. The Canada Dock is in Liverpool, L20, north of this vicinity is all Bootle, L20, which has always been a distinct Borough from Liverpool despite the close ties, and the reason why the Canada Dock and vicinity is L20 is that a portion of Kirkdale, Liverpool also comes under the postal district L20.

A bustling Liverpool landing stage photographed in 1919.

The picture on the previous page shows a busy view of the landing stage in 1919, as the *Aquitania* (31,550 tons) arrived home to be restored to a luxury liner after war service. She was built in Glasgow in 1914, and sailed from Liverpool to New York on her maiden voyage in May 1914 and this luxury Cunard Liner enjoyed 36 years on the transatlantic passenger trade, as well as seeing active war service one again during the second world war, finally meeting her fate when scrapped in 1950.

Throughout the first half of the 20th Century, liners were a common sight at the landing stage, and with Liverpool's life blood "the docks", the names of the great Liners rolled off the tongue of many scousers. Numerous ships, manned by a vast number of scousers, would ply their trade out of Liverpool to the four corners of the world, and stories galore have been passed down through generations, sadly, all too often disasters, the likes of the *Titanic*, still known to today's generation, and to a lesser extent the *Lusitania*, but of course numerous other ships lost are not so well known, particularly during the two world wars. The figure of over 29,000 merchant seamen killed on British ships during the Second World War alone, gives some indication of the loss suffered during those dark days.

The 1960s was the death knell for the great liners, the popularity of airline travel all but killed them off, the last Cunarder leaving the Mersey in 1967, just a year after the *Sylvania* sailed for the last time, marking the end of 120 years of regular transatlantic passenger services between Liverpool and New York for the Cunard Line.

The last regular liner sailing out of Liverpool was Elder Dempster's *Aureol* (14,000 tons). This shipping line traded with West Africa, and her sailing from Liverpool in March,1972 ended the wonderful era of the great liners. It was thought the liners had gone forever and no longer would people be able to stare out onto the River Mersey and be able to know what line ships belonged to by the colour of their funnels, or flags, as they sailed in and out of the port. The likes of Canadian Pacific, Cunard, Lamport and Holt, Anchor Line, Bibby Line, PSNC, Blue Funnel Line, Shaw Saville, Ellerman Line and Furness Withy amongst many others.

Yet gradually liners made a come back, particularly cruise liners, and once again, they were seen in the Mersey during the 1990s, ships such as the *QE2*, and the *Royal Viking Sun*, although they could no longer berth at the Pier Head.

This sad state of affairs became a focal point of discussion throughout the 1990s, of bringing liners back to the Pier Head. Sadly, the powers that be here in Liverpool seem to be still doing that — talking!

Finally, after years of a long drawn out battle with other ports objecting, particularly Southampton, liners are now able to turn around at the Pier Head, and although turnaround facilities are in place, a new world class berth is needed, and plans are currently on-going for such a facility.

New generations can now witness the huge liners once again, albeit not the old familiar shapes such as the *Aquitania*, and nowhere near the numbers of yesteryear, nevertheless, it's a sight to behold as the Mersey once again welcomes the liners back home.

MV Britannic III - This old postcard featuring another of the numerous Liverpool Liners, built by Harland and Wolff, she was the largest motor vessel in the world at 26,943 tons when launched on August 6th 1929, and made her maiden voyage from Liverpool to New York on June 28th 1930. She was the last of the White Star Liners, before being taken over by Cunard.

Regular fortnightly trips to New York continued with this famous old ship until her last round trip when she docked in Liverpool on December 4th 1960. As with many of her contemporaries, her final trip was to the breaker's yard, and she sailed to Inverkeithing, Scotland, in January 1961 to be scrapped.

East Princes Dock L3 - *The Liver Buildings in the distance, with the dock all but finished from its original purpose when photographed in the 1980s. Formerly the berth for the "Irish Boats" now replaced with modern buildings.*

Waterloo Dock Warehouse L3 - *Just north of the Princes Dock is the Waterloo Dock, and this photograph of the east side of the dock shows derelict warehouses in 1988, originally built in 1867, and the same view would now show luxury apartments, another example of the changing face of the dock estate over the last few decades.*

East Trafalgar Dock L3 - *Further north again, and featuring the East Trafalgar Dock, pictured in 1989, and behind the defunct dock warehouses is the former Clarence Dock power station, shortly to be demolished, the 3 chimneys long known as the three ugly sisters to generations of dock workers also demolished. Note the Liver Buildings to the right, no doubt work will soon commence on this site.*

Oceanic L3 - *Photographed in 1899, is the RMS White Star Liner,* Oceanic, *in Canada Graving Dock. She had only been launched that year from Harland and Wolff, Belfast, sadly coming to grief in 1914. She had been converted to an armed Merchant Cruiser, but sank after hitting rocks near Jutland, luckily there was no loss of life.*

Royal Iris L3 - *This more modern view from the 1980s is the* Royal Iris *in the smaller Clarence Graving Dock. Sadly, the original* Royal Iris *(known affectionately as the 'fish and chip boat') lies rotting away in London, another example of the inept attitude of our council over our maritime history. She was adored for generations by those who sailed on her on the Mersey, and instead of languishing away, she should have surely been preserved and returned as an historic attraction here in Liverpool.*

Huskisson Dock L3 - *Two ships "working" in the north 1 Huskisson Dock (left) and south 1 (right) when photographed in 1989. South 2 Huskisson Dock and north 2 Huskisson Dock no longer exist as a dock, a freighter, the* Malakand *was berthed in the south 2 branch during a particularly heavy air raid during the war, when the ship took a direct hit.*

She was loading ammunition and blown to oblivion. Several people lost their lives in that tragedy, and metal plates and other debris was found hundreds of yards away, such was the scale of the damage, and the branch dock was eventually filled in.

The north dock road (Regent Road) is now sad and desolate compared to former days, and it now terminates just before Seaforth, with the main route into/out of the City from Crosby, and through Bootle, now being known as the "Atlantic Gateway". Although still named Derby Road and Great Howard Street, many of the old buildings lining this route have been swept away, and landscaping is very much in evidence.

The decline of pubs, shops and small businesses along these major routes were ongoing when mentioned in my first publication, and this is still continuing. The decline of pubs was phenomenal, (see Lascar House) and many of the former pubs are listed in A Pub On Every Corner, Volume 3. *I said in "Tumbling Down" that the population was virtually nil, this has now been reversed, due to what was unimaginable a few decades ago, people actually living on the dock estate.*

Bibby's L3 - *A general view of the huge Bibby's complex between the dock road and Great Howard Street in the 1980s, featuring mills and warehouses, typical of the north dock road vicinity, and former status as an industrialised area; now all vanished.*

Galton Street L3 - *A lone warehouse standing derelict in Galton Street in 1989. This was in the same vicinity as Bibby's, note the Liver Building in the back ground. This was one of the last to be demolished in this vicinity, yet this old warehouse enjoyed listed status, maybe a little too early for conversion to accommodation at that time, or its location, whatever the reason, listed status did not save it.*

Lascar House L3 - *Derelict when photographed in the 1990s, last in use as an auto-kleen strainers business, when the building was named Lascar House. It was originally a pub named the Anglo American which closed in the early 1960s, the second view shows the building still standing, albeit partly demolished in 2011.*

Dominion L20 - *A rare sight along the dock road these days, a pub still standing! This view features the pub; trading in the 1920s, located at the junction with Bankfield Street. Note the statue on the top, a settler with his dog, presumably looking out to the new world. The reason I say a rare pub, is in comparative numbers from yesteryear, the second view is the side elevation of the pub from the early 1960s. Note the huge crane in the Canada Dock, despite having been closed for many years now, the building still stands..*

Canada Dock Hotel L20 - *Aptly named, as this long forgotten pub was located facing the Canada Dock, at the junction with Raleigh Street. It was listed in 1940, but not subsequently, and may have been destroyed during the war; a more modern structure now occupies this site. Incredibly, just over 100 pubs once existed along the north dock road during the 19th century. Although I refer to the dock road as such, it was actually a collection of different names, although it has always been referred to as the dock road, from town, northward they were, Goree/The Strand, (originally Back Goree) George's Dock Gates, New Quay, Bath Street, Waterloo Road, and Regent Road.*

As the docks gradually ceased working, and in turn less dockers and seamen, together with the loss of numerous other jobs connected with the docks, the pubs also declined as the 20th century progressed, and by the 1960s only 16 remained, consisting of 1 in Bath Street, 2 in Waterloo Road, and 13 in Regent Road. Currently only 4 remain open along the full length of the North dock road, (this figure can change of course).

Regent Road L20

The early view from 1998 shows the shell of the former Harland and Wolff Shipbuilding and Engineering works, a relic of the many former industries of the area, and it appeared likely to become another victim of the bulldozer. However, common sense prevailed, and as the 2003 view shows, the building was renovated, and reveals a workplace once again.

The earlier photo from 1998 is when the building was derelict. Just before going to print, early 2013, surprisingly, the building was demolished, the owners saying, "The building was unsafe, and too costly to repair". It seems strange to me that it would be unsafe just ten years after being renovated in 2003. Strange indeed!

So another part of our maritime history is gone, formerly owned by Harland and Wolff, who built the ill-fated Titanic at their Belfast yard. The White Star Cafe (on the 2003 view) refers to the White Star Line, whose headquarters were in the White Star Building (Albion House) where the Titanic was registered. It's located on the corner of The Strand and James Street, and was the first of a new generation of tall buildings when built in 1898. Sadly, despite listed status, and its prime location, the building has stood empty for some years now, as a wasted and neglected part of our maritime history (see page 218).

Luton Street L5

Featuring warehouses in Luton Street, the continuation of Boundary Street, and as featured, dating from 1861, photographed in the 1980s, prior to demolition. I wonder how many warehousemen would have trudged up those narrow winding steps over the years?

Brunswick Place L20

This photograph sums up the state of the once thriving dock road vicinity, photographed in 2003, and still the same nine years later in 2012, desolate and derelict warehouses, now relics from another age, awaiting their fate.

Sandhills Lane L5 - *This view from 2000, initially looks like a normal dock side street on a quiet sunny afternoon, with three heavy duty vehicles parked up on one side. In fact they were three abandoned wrecks, probably going unnoticed because of the location, and had been there at least 12 months! The far vehicle was a particularly large heavy duty lifting crane, and they've all since been removed, somewhat unusual for HGVs to come tumbling down!*

"Stan Waters Cafe" L3
Once a familiar name to the dock fraternity, having numerous premises throughout the dockside areas, around both the north and south docks. Derelict and awaiting demolition when photographed in 1989 pre-war it was one of the numerous pubs of the road, the Paisley Arms and was located at the junction of Great Howard Street and Paisley Street.

St Augustine's Church L3 - *This church was once part of a densely packed, and poor part of Liverpool opening in 1849 at the junction of Great Howard Street and Chadwick Street. At a time of extreme poverty, made worse by the influx of poor Irish immigrants pouring into Liverpool, approximately 16,000 people lived in this vicinity in the most squalid conditions. Conditions were no better by the 1880s, and one street in the vicinity, Carlton Street, was described as the worst street in Liverpool from a report of 1883 (a graphic description of this street's report is described in "Liverpool, our City our Heritage"). Throughout the 20th century the population began to gradually diminish from this neighbourhood. As industrialisation took over and with the population falling to virtually nil and the church finally closed in 1976. The structure remained for some time, and was in use as a builder's warehouse for a spell. This view is from 1989, and the former church was finally demolished in 1997 (see page 17).*

St Augustine's School L3 - *Featuring the school derelict when photographed in 1991, located between Upper William Street and Stone Street, having opened in 1897; in common with other inner city schools, its playground was situated on the roof. An earlier school existed, which opened in 1866, adjacent to the church, northward in Little Howard Street. It was actually a cellar, crammed between railway lines eastward, and a block of three storey dwellings and a P H, the Sarsfield Hotel, westward. It was later in use as a parish hall for the church.*

Great Howard Street L3 - *Further north along Great Howard Street, and this view from 1912 features a pub, the Stanley Arms, at the junction of Saltney Street, and the slums of the vicinity, the houses of the street fronting court property. It was about this time that the infamous courts were being cleared from the street, with a section lower down towards the dock road having already been cleared and replaced by landing houses in 1911 (see page 14). Although this property is now long gone, surprisingly, the two structures on the extreme left remain. They were two pubs, either side of Dublin Street (both featured in A Pub on every Corner, volume 3); currently one remains as a pub, with the other a café. In common with the dock road, an incredible number of pubs once traded along Great Howard Street, in its heyday over 60 once existed, the current figure is just 2 (this figure can change of course).*

Cottage L20 - *A former popular local, showing the pub derelict and about to be demolished in 1991 (an earlier view is featured in A Pub on every Corner, volume 3) this was listed as 2 Derby Road, at the junction of Boundary Street, and cleared as part of the massive scheme of widening and landscaping Great Howard Street/ Derby Road.*

Barmouth Street L5
Located off a section of Boundary Street that's known as "over the bridge" a former densely populated area when the old houses existed here. This view is from 1991, as the comparatively modern houses and maisonettes were being demolished, and the former high rise Logan Towers, built in the mid 1960s is almost cleared.

Three terraced Street's in Bootle about to bite the dust

Canal Street L20
Old terraced housing in Canal Street, off Millers Bridge, Bootle, photographed in 1969, awaiting demolition.

Berry Street L20
A section of this street remains, this portion, also off Millers Bridge, shows the old houses in the last stage of demolition from 1968.

Lamb's Terrace L 20
A small terraced street off Garden Lane, photographed during demolition in 1968, a similar terrace off Garden Lane is featured on page 16.

The three previous photographs are all from the late 1960s, and over four decades later, another three streets are awaiting demolition in Bootle.

In common with other areas such as Anfield and Granby, decline has gone on for years, as uncertainty over demolition or renovation gradually leaves rows of streets in an ever spiral of deterioration as people move out, and the vandals move in, and in early 2012, demolition does seem likely, yet policies do change, and it will be beyond the scope of this book as to what will eventually happen.

Arvon Street off Springwell Road L20

Edith Road off Monfa Road L20

Menai Road off Monfa Road L20

Just a short distance away used to be the so called "Klondyke" estate, which has recently been cleared, with new housing already being built so named after the nick-name of William Jones, a Welsh builder who came to Liverpool in the 1860s. After building houses in Everton and Toxteth, he turned to Bootle, first building houses off Irlam Road, then his most well known "Klondyke" estate off Hawthorne Road.

The three previous streets are in the Orrell district of Bootle, a former "Parish" that was incorporated into Bootle-cum-Linacre in 1905. Many such "parishes" or "townships" existed in west Lancashire, north of Liverpool, until the 1970s, as new boundaries were created as part of a reorganisation of local government, and in 1974 the new Metropolitan Borough of Sefton was formed, (itself a former parish) becoming one of the new boroughs that form part of Merseyside.

On a personal note, I would have preferred the phrase "Greater Liverpool" or "Liverpool region" as outside of England the name Merseyside is all but unknown, far better to have had Liverpool in the title, as it's known worldwide.

Orrell Presbyterian Church L20

Standing derelict in this vicinity at the junction of Springwell Road and Church Road when photographed in 2012, a church and pub may not have much in common, except as indicated throughout this publication, their demise is all too common, as numerous have, and still continue to be demolished throughout the inner City areas over the years. Before going to print, I believe plans to renovate this former church are ongoing, so obviously outside the scope of this book as to its fate.

Off Vauxhall Road
(1986)

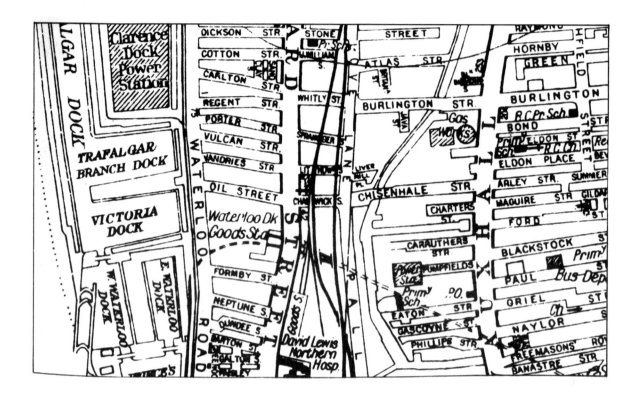

After the mass demolition of housing in the 1960s, it could be said that the early 1980s was the age of mass demolition of factories. The combined effects of Liverpool's steady decline as a port and the mass unemployment of the current recession is symbolised in the Vauxhall Road area quite simply as the wholesale demolition of factories and warehouses. The dramatic demolition of the huge Tate and Lyle sugar refinery plant in 1983 was taken to be the end of an entire chapter of Liverpool's history. Sugar has been an important part of Liverpool's trade since the seventeenth century. There was refinery in Liverpool as early as 1670, close to Redcross Street in the city centre. The huge Tate & Lyle plant began its life in the 1870s and operated for over a hundred years. The decline of trade in other commodities, such as tobacco, which were also related to Britain's imperial past has also severely affected Liverpool.

Vauxhall Road's reputation as home for an exceedingly large number of pubs is mostly a thing of the past too. Many have been demolished, though it is interesting to note that they are often the last buildings to be cleared on a particular site as breweries are always reluctant to lose licensed premises.

The large number of pubs is a reflection of the density of the population in the nineteenth century. In 1847 Chisenhale Street, only 334 yards long, contained no less than 19 separate courts as well as several early 'landing' blocks. The earliest of these mean courts were given wholly unsuitable, pretty names such as Priscilla Court, Rose Court and Rebecca Court. However, such was the scale of their proliferation that subsequent ones bear only a number or a letter as their identification in the densely populated street.

Typical of the life of the old area was the story told to me many times by my dad about the old 'Lock Fields'. Well known in the district years ago, 'Lock Fields' was simply a field near Vauxhall Road and the locks of the Leeds-Liverpool canal. When my dad was a young man this was the place where men would fight each other in the morning, often after an argument in one of the local pubs the night before. The custom was that instead of fighting there and then, they would meet the next morning on the Lock Fields. Hundreds of spectators from the area would be there to watch. Another aspect of old Liverpool now long forgotten.

The only building left standing on the Chisenhale Street is the public house called the 'Bridge', logically enough perhaps as it stands on the bridge over the famous Leeds and Liverpool canal. Its less prestigious local nickname however is 'The Flyhouse'.

The large, half demolished warehouse which is shown on the right of the photograph adjoined Tate and Lyles. It dated from 1847 but even its listed building status failed to save it.

Seen by many Liverpudlians as a symbol of the destruction of the city's industry during the current recession, the massive Tate and Lyle refinery was undergoing demolition in 1983.

This warehouse dated from 1872 and was also associated with the sugar refining industry which was reaching its peak at that time.

Tiny terraced houses in Arley Street off the eastern side of Vauxhall Road which have long since vanished. There were no windows at all to the rear of this terrace. The author photographed by younger brother Ray in 1967.

'Scotch Houses' in Arley Street. Note the four doors in a row leading to two upstairs and two downstairs one roomed 'bed sitting rooms'.

Eldon Place, adjoining Arley Street has another type of dwelling familiar in the old Liverpool slums. The cramped two-up two-down houses with cellars were cleared in the late 1960s along with most of the rest of the area.

The junction of Vauxhall Road and Burlington Street was the site of this warehouse until demolition in 1981. The road was notorious for the large number of pubs it contained, two of which can clearly be seen here.

Burlington Street, off Vauxhall Road, had the characteristic 'landing' houses which were built in many parts of Liverpool in the decade before the First World War to replace the terrible slums of the nineteenth century. They were considered a great improvement at that time and are clearly forerunners of the municipal flats of the inter-war period. This block was demolished in 1970.

Burlington Street also has examples of municipal tenements from different periods. On the left stand flats from the 1920s which are still occupied today. Portland Gardens on the right of the road are from the 1930s and these are undergoing renovation. The chimney of the Tate and Lyle refinery is visible in the background during demolition in 1983.

A typical block of early twentieth century 'landing' houses in St. Silvester Place just prior to demolition in 1966.

This was the first municipal housing in the country, St Martin's Cottages stood in Silvester Street. Erected in 1869 they should surely have been preserved, if not renovated for continued habitation.

Boundary Street at the end of Kirkdale Road is so named because it was the ancient boundary between Liverpool and Kirkdale. These listed Georgian buildings were built around 1830, still standing but in obvious need of repair.

Around Scottie Road
(1986)

Scotland Road runs along what was once the old coach route to the north from the town centre. But the rural scenery changed dramatically in the nineteenth century as the commerce and industry of a major sea port created workshops, pubs and doss-houses and tens of thousands of poorly built, cramped houses in the narrow streets and courts off the main highway. Its name became – and still is for many people – synonymous with Liverpool, epitomising both the best and the worst, depending on your view point, of the city's attributes. The squalor and strife that existed here from early Victorian times was never quite eradicated. Despite successive waves of demolition and considerable bomb damage during the last war it was still amongst the worst areas of housing in the 1960s. Yet I know I am not alone in believing that here amongst the poor conditions there was as much humour and pride as there was poverty and defeat – just like any working class community in the north. These things are no less true despite having been turned into clichés by being so frequently observed. My memory, certainly, insists that the front door steps glistened from the constant rubbing with sandstone blocks and almost every family boasted at least one 'character' and several natural comedians! I remember one such character, Thomas Gately. A docker for 46 years, he grew up in the mean courts off Scotland Road. He was a distant relative, but to me more like a grandfather. Like so many dockland characters he was best known by his nickname. In fact over the years he had two nicknames. Before the war people called him 'The Quiet Man' – because he talked so much! After the war he became known as 'The Lone Ranger', because of his habit of collecting pieces of silver paper. He amassed sacks full over the years to raise money for charity. 'Gate' as he was known to his close friends was full of odd comic rhymes and sayings. Amongst my most abiding memory of Gate was, if I was ever a 1d or 2d short for the pictures (which was sometimes funded by taking back empty jam jars for 1d refund), he would always give me the coppers saying his immortal line "Come back when yer 21".

The Scottie Road area is full of such memories for me when I was born on Hopwood Street just off Scotland Road. These streets were our playground until we moved in the 1950s.

My brothers and I spent much of our childhood in the streets and alleys of the district. One of our favourite games in those days was to turn one of the old gas lamps into a swing. We would sway about wildly hanging onto an old car tyre suspended from a rope lashed to the cross bar.

During the 1960s, the whole Scotland Road area began to change beyond recognition particularly with the building of the second Mersey Tunnel. Scottie Road itself has been greatly reduced. The frontage has completely disappeared from the start of Byrom Street to the original Mersey Tunnel with just the section from the tunnel northward to the Rotunda remaining of this once notorious hub of old Liverpool. The Rotunda was a former theatre that stood at the junction of Scotland Road and Stanley Road and the name is still commonly used for this junction.

Scotland Road. This block adjoining the Corner House pub on Scotland Road dates from the 1840s and was demolished in 1983 leaving the pub in isolation.

The west side of Scotland Road, near Bevington Hill, was demolished in the late 1960s.

The 'Westmoreland Arms Scotland Road, known locally as the 'Honky Tonk' bears an inscription which reads "One of Liverpool's oldest pubs established in 1740." The adjoining block has since been renovated. In the background stands Woodstock Gardens awaiting demolition.

Ashfield Gardens off the western side of Scotland Road awaiting demolition in 1983.

Woodstock Gardens were typical pre-war municipal flats, shown here awaiting demolition in 1983. Visible through the arch is St Anthony's Church, Scotland Road, built in 1833.

The Ship established in 1858, was at the corner of Latimer Street and Hopwood Street and was still open for business in 1983 when it was gutted by fire.

The Globe' another of Scottie Road's old pubs, at the corner of Woodstock Street was closed in 1969 and demolished soon after.

These 'landing' houses in Hornby Street were built in the early 1900s to replace older slums; they were themselves demolished at the end of the 1960s.

*An old block of houses including a former stable on Limekiln Lane at the corner of
Tatlock Street. The League of Welldoers Club now occupies this site.*

*Three storey houses undergoing demolition on Norris Street in 1967,
the central door provided the entrance to the inner court.*

Louis Street and Taliesen Street off the eastern side of Scotland Road were typical streets of the area. The 3 storey houses in Taliesen Street had no rear windows at all.

Victoria Square, built in the 1880s was an ambitious scheme to replace the horrific slums of the nineteenth century. The five storey tenement blocks contained 282 flats and won an architectural award for their advanced design when first erected. The photograph shows its demolition in 1966.

Scotland Road/Vauxhall L3, L5

Once amongst the most dense slum ridden hovels in Liverpool during the 19th Century, and into the 20th Century, as described in this publication, the worst hovels were the former "courts" and cellars, now thankfully wiped out completely. In the 1840s, 2,400 existed, in which some 38,000 people lived, although greatly reduced in numbers, they were still in abundance by the 1930s, and it was not until the 1960s when they were finally consigned to history.

To tackle the appalling slums of Victorian Liverpool a gradual improvement started with the construction of St Martins Cottages, although it wasn't till the 1890s that it was tackled in earnest. After the "housing of the working classes act of 1890" the following gives some insight of previous housing schemes to combat the appalling slums of this area, over the decades.

Eldon Street L3 - *These dwellings were built in 1905, and were a new conception at the time, having been built with reinforced concrete panels by renowned City Engineer, Alexander Brodie, who was in office from 1898 to 1925. Yet somewhat strangely, it didn't take off as a new venture, as the next large scheme in this vicinity during 1911, and 1912, did not continue with the idea. Note most of the children in their "Sunday best" with a few barefoot children amongst them. (see page 57)*

Argyll Place L5

A variation of "landing houses" which were mainly built in the early 20th century, formerly located between Tatlock Street, and Raymond Street, off Vauxhall Road. An adjacent block is on page 43 whereas another variation from the 1920s, Holly Street, is featured on page 150.

Eldon Grove L3

Part of one of the largest schemes of slum clearance after the 1890 Act occurred in the Bevington Street vicinity, of which this was part, and was completed in 1911, and in my Pub book, volume 3, I stated it's future was uncertain, featuring a 1997 photograph of the block boarded up. They were briefly 'done up' then in 1999, as this view shows, once again empty, and similar schemes have since occurred. Currently they are still standing once again derelict, but I hope they will be preserved once and for all, as they are now a very rare example of this type of property, but with Liverpool's record of demolition it may be wishful thinking.

Two ornate cast iron street lamps stand here, and are actually "listed". Sadly listed status doesn't guarantee structures being preserved, and on this view the neglect is all too obvious, they once had two drinking fountains on each side, and a Liver Bird also adorned the top, since removed.

The 1930s era produced "landing" houses on a new scale, 4 or 5 storey tenement blocks, and no longer had railings on the landings. They were built throughout the City and were most prevalent in this and the Dingle area. Many were inappropriately named "gardens" for despite the improvement from previous living conditions, greenery was one thing lacking. New garden housing estates were also constructed in this era, notably the Speke and Norris Green areas.

The following tenements are from this era

Vauxhall Gardens L3

Formerly located west of Vauxhall Road, and south of Leeds Street, this view is from 1987, shortly before demolition. Modern housing is now abundant in this area; note the "three ugly sisters" in the distance, (that was the nick-name given to the chimneys of the former Clarence Dock Power Station, featured in the dock section).

Fontenoy Gardens L3

Also photographed in 1987, they were located in Fontenoy Street, adjacent to Byrom Street, with new housing now covering this site, the "wall" shown in this view is part of the vent of the old Waterloo tunnel, a former railway cutting that led from Waterloo Dock to Edge Hill, similar to the Wapping tunnel (Wapping Dock to Edge Hill).

For years there has been talk of opening one, or both of them again, either for railway traffic, or road traffic, but sadly just talk, nothing has ever materialised, and they remain a wasted and neglected part of underground Liverpool.

Another tunnel that still exists in Edge Hill is the Crown Street tunnel, a date of 1829 is still visible inside the tunnel, and iron railings now at its end; beyond, modern houses this was the terminus for the first passenger railway in the world, Crown Street but sadly, unlike its counterpart in Manchester, the terminus here was demolished for houses, with no thought of preservation.

Lawrence Gardens L3
Formerly located in Lawrence Street, adjacent to Victoria Square, east of Scotland Road, photographed in 1975, when in an advanced state of demolition.

Chaucer House L3
A gas lamp still lit in Ellenborough Street, off Scotland Road, pictured here in 1969 shortly before demolition, the tenemants were on the east side of Scotland Road, between Chaucer Street and Juvenal Street. The second view shows the landings on the other side of the block, this, and the previous view, is now part of the approach road to the Kingsway tunnel.

Ashfield Gardens L5
Located west of Scotland Road, this view is from the corner of Latimer Street when photographed in 1983; adjacent stood Hopwood Gardens, and to make a trio of tenements, Woodstock Gardens was also in this vicinity, all now long demolished, (Woodstock Gardens is on page 47).

Despite all the previous views being improvements to former living conditions, they themselves eventually became victim to the bulldozer, and the following are just four of the slums the previous type of housing replaced, now mainly eradicated from living memory.

Arley Street L3 - *These tenements were known as "Scotch Houses" unlike the two-up two-down type of houses still frequently found in Liverpool. They consisted of two and three rooms, note they had four front doors adjacent, with the two centre ones leading to separate rooms upstairs, photographed c.1904 (a 1960s view is on page 41).*

Eldon Street L3 - *The slums here shown as court entrances to numbers 5, 7, and 9 courts, and was also photographed c.1904. This was part of the huge slum clearance area in the Bevington Street area, with a block built in 1905 in this street (shown on page 51).*

Burlington Street L3

Originally running from Scotland Road westward to Love Lane, and was 859 yards long, with the section over Vauxhall Road now part of the Eldonian Village; this view is from 1926, again court property between the houses. Some of the old courts were simply numbered, such as the previous view; whereas some where named such as this street, the first one named Devon Place. Note the cellars bricked up on the first block, with others still open, and although illegal by this period, people would have certainly still lived in them. Two budgie cages are outside the first house for fresh air, yet somewhat strangely, no more are visible, obviously photographed on a summers day.

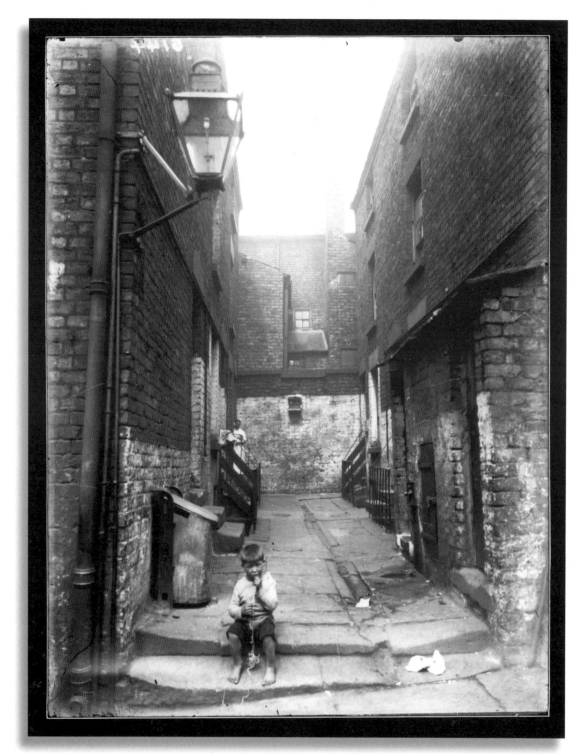

Byrom Street L3

Another "named" court, this was Cartwright Place, looking into the court itself, and showing a barefoot street urchin inquisitively looking at the camera man when photographed in 1927. Despite the progress made with housing in the inter-war years, with the coming of the Second World War, and its aftermath, the housing situation was actually worse than before the War because of the Luftwaffe, with over 6,000 houses and flats destroyed, and over 125,000 damaged.

In the post-war years one of the first schemes to combat the chronic shortage of housing was the construction of temporary prefabricated bungalows, or as they were known, "prefabs". 3,500 were built on some 40 sites across the City, and although temporary, they lasted for years, still abundant in the 1960s. During the 1950s, high rise flats appeared (see Everton) and with the situation so bad immediately after the war, flats based on the 1930s type were constructed, in various parts of the City including the following two examples.

Highfield Gardens L3
Located close to the previous mentioned Vauxhall Gardens, and built between 1947 - 1949, and extended through to Upper Milk Street, and this view from 1987 had people still living in them prior to eventual demolition.

Portland Gardens L3
Formerly located off the south side Burlington Street, with the north side and Portland Street containing similar tenements, built at the same time as the previous block, and by the 1980s such property was becoming obsolete, and this view from 1986 shows the scaffolding going up for their demolition.

Crompton Street/Athol Street area L5

Continuing the demolition theme, I am now featuring housing being cleared from the last decade of the 20th Century, and still ongoing after the new millennium, although not slums as the previous views, but comparatively modern houses, albeit some were definitely "jerry" built.

Although this is the Compton Street/Athol Street vicinity, they are by no means on their own. Such property has been demolished City wide, from construction in the 1950s, and each decade thereafter into the new millennium, as flats, houses, and maisonettes have been, or are still to be demolished. The estates built in the inter-war years are in a similar situation. Once desirable houses in the likes of Norris Green and Speke are now often lying derelict and inhospitable, although long overdue improvements are currently in progress in both estates, which should have happened a decade or so earlier. On top of this numerous terraced houses from the 19th Century still exist, many of them also derelict and decayed.

Why has this come about? Complicated of course, amenities such as running water, gas and electricity, were unknown in most of the properties these houses replaced, although such things are taken for granted nowadays. Architects and developers bear the brunt of the blame, with the likes of "rabbit hutch" houses having been built for some decades now, and even into the new millennium many new houses are still far too small. Lack of maintenance by the council is another, and private landlords over the years is yet another candidate, even changing attitudes, in fact as stated, it's very complicated, but from a personal point of view I suspect one of the prime reasons is not so much the actual houses, but society, namely a scourge of modern times — anti-social behaviour. This action caused by rampaging youths and even children does actually bring whole areas down, literally! It only takes one empty house to be destroyed by vandals, and the situation snowballs so that more and more people leave, as more and more houses become vandalised, eventually leaving the area devastated.

This appalling situation still continues, as I know only too well, because I live in one such area, a corner of Anfield that not so long ago was a pleasant area to live, but for some years has declined on a seemingly never ending spiral because of anti-social behaviour, resulting in ever more derelict burnt out houses as people moved away. (see Rockfield Road, Anfield). Fortunately, anti-social behaviour is taken more seriously nowadays, and in my neck of the woods has stabilised somewhat, although empty properties continue to blight the vicinity, and many other communities across the City.

It's appalling that into the second decade of a new millennium so much property both old and new is so run down throughout the City, but it's not all doom and gloom of course, the likes of the Eldonian estate is a success story. Many of the 1960s estates since rebuilt are also successful such as the Queen's Road estate in Everton, and Cantril Farm on the outskirts, since renamed Stockbridge Village.

The remainder of this section contains various locations as follows:

Vauxhall Road/Marybone L3
The pace of change into the new millennium in the City Centre and fringes can well be illustrated by the following two views photographed from Tithebarn Street. The corner block was a well known landmark for years, containing a small garage at street level, whilst the adjoining block on Vauxhall Road was in the process of demolition when photographed in 2000.

The second view is the same location photographed barely three years later, in 2003, the huge corner block almost completed, and an even higher block of student accommodation well on the way to completion in Marybone.

Queens Arms PH L3 - *Like the dock road, and Great Howard Street, Vauxhall Road also had pubs galore along its length, particularly during the 19th Century, then a densely populated and highly industrialised area. Around 70 existed at its peak, and in common with all thoroughfares, they diminished over the years, together with industry. By the 1960s only 12 pubs remained, and currently 4 are trading (this can change of course) and this particular one, formerly listed at 41 Vauxhall Road ceased trading in the late 1950s, and now long demolished; the street corner on which it stood was Northampton Street - demolished. The photograph c.1912.*

Tate and Lyle sugar refinery L3 - *Looking more like the blitz than 1983, as the last remnants of the former sugar refinery is demolished (see page 40) where I said it was seen by many Liverpudlians as a symbol of the destruction of the City's industry, and to a certain extent is still true today. The site is now part of the highly acclaimed Eldonian Village.*

Vauxhall Road L5 - *Although Tate and Lyle's was the most well known sugar refinery, others also existed in Liverpool such as the one featured in this view, Fairrie's (the name partly shown on the extreme left). "They don't build things like they used to" is a common phrase heard nowadays, and is certainly true in many cases, and this former refinery is a perfect example, the section in the forefront about to be demolished looking more like a Castle battlement than a refinery!*

The adjoining scrap yard was also shortly to go when photographed in the 1980s, as the demise of Vauxhall Road's once thriving industry comes tumbling down. This refinery dated 1847, was listed, although as with so many other listed structures, the "listed status" did not save them. (see page 39 for a view looking in the opposite direction).

Ship Hotel L5 - *Located in the same area as the previously mentioned Crompton Street/Athol Street section, this pub was at the junction of Hopwood Street and Latimer Street, and was photographed in the 1950s when the old housing still remained in both streets. For a later view when the pub remained in isolation after the old streets were demolished see page 47.*

Burroughs Gardens L3

Showing Burroughs Gardens baths, at the junction of Limekiln Lane, in the 1980s. They opened in 1877, and would have been a wonderful amenity at that time, especially for the poor, when water was still a scarce commodity. Westminster Road baths in Kirkdale also opened in the same year.

Arden Street L3

A former well-known landmark of the area, the Salvation Army hostel in Arden House; the street was only 68 yards long from Scotland Road to Bevington Bush. Photographed when empty and awaiting demolition in 1986.

Scotland Place L3 - *Photographed in the 1950s, this separated Byrom Street from Scotland Road, and originally contained the largest brewery in the town when operational in the 1790s, Porter's Brewery. Three pubs are featured, on the right - the Dunbar Castle, at the junction of Byrom Street and Circus Street - the one in the centre the Birmingham Arms on Richmond Row, and on the left the Morning Star. The shop adjoining the Birmingham Arms was formerly known in the area, as the "98 shop" referring to the 1798 rebellion in Ireland. All the property in this view are now long gone, with Scotland Place consigned to history.*

Taliesen Street/Louis Street L5 - *A "headless" gas light dominating this view during demolition in 1967. Located off Scotland Road looking towards Great Homer Street, Taliesen Street was an early type of terraced property having no back windows; two separate views are shown on page 50.*

Derby Cinema L5

One of the few buildings still standing on Scotland Road that has yet to succumb to the bulldozer. Originally built as a Wesleyan Chapel, then a Methodist Free Church prior to its conversion to a cinema in 1912, it finally closed in 1960, having a variety of uses since closure, notably a funeral parlour, and is currently vacant. Another cinema on Scotland Road was the Gaiety, (a popular venue for my parents in their "courting days"). This too closed at the same time in 1960, whereas a short lived cinema was the Electric Theatre, well beyond living memory. In the early 20th century, operating from 1911 to 1921, the former cinema's name (The Derby) is still displayed on the view from 2011.

Scotland Road L3

Years ago Scotland Road boasted more pubs than any other thoroughfare in Liverpool and are all documented in volume four of A Pub On Every Corner. *Therefore I am just featuring this one in particular, as it surely must have had the most unusual name of any pub in Liverpool, or the country for that matter, having the remarkable title, "the Faugh-a-Ballagh".*

In volume four, I said the name was never actually verified, although one source claimed it was apparently derived from a Munster Irish Regiment which was disbanded in 1916. That was almost correct, as the origin of the name was actually a "battle cry" from the 1790s and was eventually adopted by an Irish Regiment. The photograph is from the 1890s, and pre 1860s it was named the Dog & Partridge, then the Shamrock around the turn of the century before going back to its original name, the Dog & Partridge, possibly in an effort to keep trading. However it closed in the late 1920s, and is refered to as Dining Rooms in the 1930s. In common with many main thoroughfares of the City, Scotland Road's pubs have been closing down for years, along with houses and shops with the construction of the Kingsway, Mersey tunnel, which opened in 1971. This trend continued to accelerate over the last few decades, ever rising costs and dwindling population being the main factors for local pubs closing. Then a major blow was the smoking ban, in small locals particularly, who unlike larger pubs could not provide a smoking area, and this trend goes on relentlessly. Currently only three remain on Scotland Road, all with bird named connections. They are the Throstle's Nest, Eagle Vaults, and the Parrot, although the latter is currently closed. This figure can change, of course, and one of the few shops still trading on the road, a butchers, was originally a pub long before living memory, trading before the First World War as the Prince of Wales Vaults.

Kirkdale across to Walton
(1986)

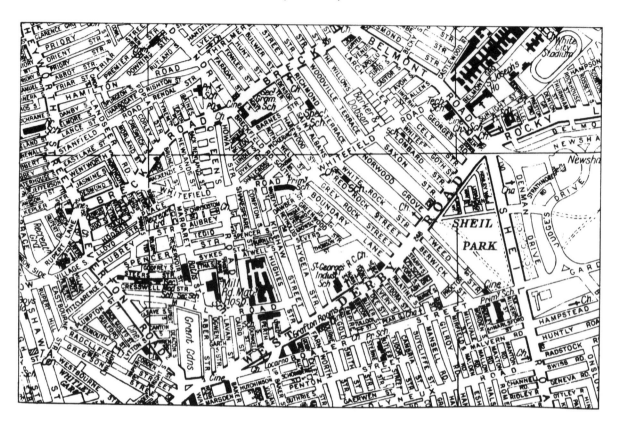

Stanley Road in Kirkdale is the long major road which runs from the Rotunda at Scotland Road northwards into Bootle. Before it reaches Bootle it passes through the heart of Kirkdale. This was my dad's old neighbourhood, he was born in Blackfield Street. This area holds many memories from my childhood when I used to visit my Auntie Kath in Lambeth Road. Despite warnings I would sneak down notorious Reading Street and watch the gangs of men playing cards behind the tenements. These card games were known as 'toss schools' and were an important, though usually secretive, form of entertainment for many men in the pre-television era of the 1950s. To get to Auntie Kath's I used to catch a tram from Sleeper's Hill to Lambeth Road. Sleeper's Hill was also the starting point for our gang when we travelled on a tram, perhaps to the 'distant' country at Spinney Woods in Kirkby. The adventure of trams was never quite matched when they were replaced by buses in 1956. Nevertheless a ride on a new bus to far off places such as Otterspool was still magical. It always seems such a shame that the variety of colours of the buses, yellow in Wallasey or blue in Birkenhead, has gone and a uniform green is the order of today. The operation of the buses has also been transformed since those days. I drove a bus myself for seven years when the full 'crew' included a conductor and the job was more interesting and often hilarious. Many of the conductors were jovial and helpful to their passengers but sadly this personal aspect of the job diminished greatly when they were replaced by today's driver-only operation.

Stanley Park, on the border of Anfield, holds the key to the warmest recollections, where with countless other children I would spend hours playing during the Summer months. The tiny row of shops shown in the photograph in this section was directly opposite the swings in the park. When we had money (usually a penny) we would go over there for an incredible choice of riches – a lolly ice, a penny 'Vantas' drink or, a favourite in those days, an 'Arrow' bar. Alongside the park swings was a 'show', a wooden shed with a raised stage. From time to time a clown, ventriloquist or similar act would appear and a large queue of kids would be waiting with their threepenny "Joey's" (3d piece) to get in. For those with no money there were always the trees for the grandstand view. The children themselves often got up on the stage and I remember one day in 1958 my brother Frank and friend Paul Waters got up on stage and sang an Everley Brother's song to tremendous applause, (my older brother Jackie and our gang had 'persuaded' the other children to clap for our kid).

Stanley Park was the first park in Liverpool to have an open air swimming bath and it was extremely popular. At times there would be droves of us from the streets in our neighbourhood around Blessington Road converging on the baths with our bottles of water and 'jam butties'. Sadly the baths and the 'show' no longer exist. They are now just a wonderful memory. Gone too are the rowing boats. The little hut where we would pay sixpence to hire a boat is still standing but it is extensively vandalised. The only other reminder is the small jetty where the boats were tied up.

This substantial, well-constructed block on Stanley Road at the junction with Lambeth Road, shows the red engineering brick characteristic of much of this area.

Brighton Terrace in Stanley Road was unusual for its elevated position, now demolished.

Flinders Street, off Commercial Road, was typical of a great number of terraces built from the 1860s. The site is now a football pitch and all of the surrounding streets have been cleared. This part of Kirkdale is presently a wilderness and post-war housing too is being demolished.

Reading Street became a notorious street in Liverpool with some of the earliest of the tenement buildings dating from the mid-nineteenth century. The last sections were not finally cleared until the early 1960s, many of the former residents being rehoused in Kirkby.

Elstow Street, adjoining Reading Street, contained very poor terraced housing. By the time it was demolished in 1977. Tillotsons factory, visible in the background on Commercial Road, was then derelict.

Great Mersey Street, off Stanley Road was one of the early streets of rural Kirkdale village. At the junction with Smith Street stood a Victorian pub, The Britannia flanked on both sides by earlier housing. Virtually all this block was demolished in the early 70s.

Blackfield Street. These early nineteenth century terraces with front gardens would have been on the very edge of town and much sought after when first built. The once attractive street has been replaced by a new housing development.

Brisbane Street, off Smith Street, illustrates another type of two storey terrace. The special features of these small houses was that they had windows at the rear on the upper floor only. (See below left)

Seen here from Latham Street, a rear view of the unusual construction of the terraced houses in Brisbane Street.

3 storey mid-Victorian terrace in Vesuvius Street, shown here in dereliction in 1966.

Another variation on a familiar theme, this 'landing' house block in Smith Street had central stairs for access to the upper floors. The building faced Whittle Street which itself contained many similar ones dating from the 1890s.

At the junction of Smith Street and Kirkdale Road stood this massive well-built public house with interesting decorative brickwork. The site of the Goats Head *is now landscaped.*

Westminster Road Baths are still standing although the original frontage of 1876 was demolished along with many other adjacent properties when a new road scheme, now abandoned, was planned for this once busy main thoroughfare.

This small block of back-to-back houses, Church Terrace, stood in Archer Street, off Westminster Road. It was opposite St Mary's Church which was built in 1835. The terrace and the church – once a part of rural Kirkdale before the adjoining industrial city overran it – were demolished in the early 1970s.

This early Victorian terrace was situated in the gentle curve of Sessions Road – aptly named as it originally led to old Kirkdale jail, around 1819. This photograph from 1967 shows the houses in considerable decay.

A pub bearing the old name The Elm Tree stands on this ground, but not the one shown here which was demolished in 1978. The site at Westminster Road and Barlow Lane junction is believed to be an ancient site of many former inns. This junction is one of the original lanes that led to the old villages of Walton and Bootle.

Small, mid-Victorian terraced houses of four rooms plus cellars stood in Whitefield Lane. This narrow lane is now part of the site of a housing estate built in the late 1970s. The immediate vicinity of Westminster Road contained some fine Victorian houses alongside these poor terraces.

Fonthill House, Melrose Road was one of four tenement blocks built in 1923. They were demolished in 1983 whilst identical blocks of the same period still stand in the Dingle, south of the City.

This unusual block of terraced houses built above a row of tiny shops stood on Walton Lane opposite Stanley Park. This scene is from 1964.

This substantial Victorian terrace at the junction of Walton Lane and Alexander Square should surely have been renovated. New housing now stands here following demolition of the original buildings in the early 1970s.

Walton Road, formerly one of Liverpool's main shopping districts is now sad and desolate.

Walton Road boasted many fine pubs. One recent sad closure was the Penrhyn Castle.

Stanley Park lake with the jetty and boat hiring hut, sadly no longer in use.

Updated

Kirkdale Across to Walton

Boundary Street L5

So named as it was the ancient boundary between Liverpool and Kirkdale. Listed buildings were extremely rare in north Liverpool, and the Georgian houses of this street were an example. In 1986 I featured this street, and ended the commentary with "but in obvious need of repair". That never happened, they were allowed to deteriorate, and with a little help from the weather and vandals they were soon beyond repair, and this view is from the 1980s as they were being demolished (See page 43).

Sellar Street L4 - *Large scale demolition in the Lambeth Road area occurred in 2011, this view showing a street sign left in isolation, and new houses are currently replacing the 1970s stock.*

Lambeth Walk L4 - *Also photographed in 2011, and was the last of the 1970s built houses off the north side of Lambeth Road awaiting demolition, and since cleared.*

The following four photographs show the changing face of Kirkdale Road

Crown Vaults L5 - *Displaying Ind Coope & Allsopp, Brewers, who were later taken over by Allied Breweries Ltd, when photographed in the 1950s, and is listed number 25, at the junction of Wrexham Street, whose old houses can be seen on the right, whereas the old frontage of three storey shops still remains.*

Crown Vaults L5 - *The same pub in 2000 with new houses by then on Wrexham Street, and the old three storey frontage replaced by typical 1970s flats, and at that time, with the pub derelict, it would appear its days were numbered.*

Remainder of the 1970s flats L5 - *In the same year, the flats themselves now empty, awaiting demolition. They stretched to Great Mersey Street and were demolished shortly after this view.*

Crown Vaults L5 - *As shown, the pub somehow avoided the bulldozer, and this view from 2011 also shows modern houses where the flats stood. The pub is now the only old structure remaining on Kirkdale Road, and although still trading, it currently has a 'For sale' sign. The road originally had twelve pubs, and the following two were on the stretch of the road between here and Great Mersey Street before the old property was demolished.*

Castle PH L5
Previously numbered 51, at the junction of Lancaster Street, and demolished in the 1960s.

Mersey Hotel L5
Standing at the end of the block, numbered 61, and 170 Great Mersey Street, this early view c1905. Note the ornate gas lamp on the right, outside a former gents' toilet, once common on the streets of the City. The previous pub can partly be seen along the road, and this pub was also demolished in the 1960s.

The following three short streets were to be found between Latham Street and Back Great Mersey Street in the 1960s

Vesuvius Street L5
This was 118 yards long, but unlike the following two, these were large three storey houses. Another view of this street is on page 71 which was also photographed in 1966.

Pluto Street L5
Photographed in 1968, only 121 yards long, and this view during demolition is looking towards Latham Street; note this terrace had small front gardens.

Sterling Street L5 - *Also photographed in 1968, with a gas light still lit despite daylight, also with small front gardens. This was 109 yards long.*

Smith Street L5 - *A block of early landing houses shown on page 72 occupied this site in the 1960s. Although they were demolished as "slum" dwellings, their replacement, built in the 1970s, could well be classed as a "modern slum" - jerry built houses - common throughout the City in the era, and this view of their demolition is from 2003, after being an eyesore for some years.*

Union P H L5
A lone pub standing at the junction of Commercial Road and Sandhills Lane when photographed in 1995. The surrounding factories, pubs, and streets off Commercial Road had long been demolished by then; the pub also known as Lowe's and was demolished in 1997.

For many years now the supermarkets and out of town shopping malls have gradually wiped out the small shopkeepers, inevitable really, as when the old terraced streets were in abundance, the main roads they were off were lined with mainly three storey blocks of shops, which catered for all the needs of the locals, and as the streets disappeared so did many of the frontage blocks. Kirkdale Road, previously mentioned is an example, just one building left, many others have all but been wiped out, such as Great Howard Street, Netherfield Road North, Great Homer Street, West Derby Road (the Liverpool 6 section) Islington, and Park Road.

A lot do remain of course, the likes of County Road, Kensington and Smithdown Road for example. Nowadays the majority, sadly, have numerous empty shops amongst those still trading. The following are three such blocks from Stanley Road.

Stanley Road L5
A substantial block consisting of red glazed brick, the likes of which certainly won't be built again. This was located on the west side of the road, between Lambeth Road and Aspinall Street, and photographed in 1981, shortly before demolition; another view is on page 69.

Stanley Road L5
This 1950s view is of the block between Lambeth Road and Reading Street now long demolished, although the corner pub, the Lighthouse, remains in isolation, having opened and closed on a number of occasions in recent years, and currently closed.

Stanley Road L20
Another example of a whole block awaiting demolition when photographed in 2003 all the shops being empty. Formerly on the east side of the road between Celia Street and Argos Road, although in L20, it was still in Liverpool as described in the north dock section.

Lemon Street L5 - *Just one of the many former streets of old terraced property off Commercial Road and vicinity, all now long gone; this view is from 1968, shortly before demolition.*

Reading Street L5
Early landing houses off Stanley Road, photographed during demolition in the early 1960s, the rear of the houses are on Lambeth Road, which still remain, whereas the other side, and numerous streets were demolished from the 1960s. Strange how just one side of Lambeth Road survived, beyond the former landing houses and a number of streets also still stand, known collectively as the flower streets due to their names. A separate view of Reading Street is on page 70.

St Alphonsus L5
With the old community gone, and so the population greatly reduced, the local parish church also becomes redundant, sadly the price of progress, as numerous churchs have followed the same fate. Standing in Great Mersey Street, and photographed in 2001, as the demolition is almost complete.

Orwell Road / Sessions Road L4 - *Featuring a pub, the Sessions, formerly listed 145 Orwell Road and 91 Sessions Road, originally named the Court House Hotel, and both names are in connection with the old Kirkdale Jail (1819) which stood on the land behind the pub (a more comprehensive history of the jail is in* Liverpool Our City Our Heritage*). The tower block shown during demolition in 1999, was named Brockmoor Tower, and the pub has also since been demolished.*

Humber Street L4 - *Formerly located between Medlock Street and Leven Street in the Orwell Road area, photographed in 1976, shortly before demolition; more modern houses now abundant in the area.*

Harlech Street L4 - *Only the entrance left from a former tram, then bus sheds, photographed in 1999; a bingo hall now covers part of this site. The pub beyond the sheds, the Carisbrooke, is still trading to date.*

Derby Arms Hotel L4 - *Formerly numbered 2 Walton Road, at the junction of Everton Valley, a large flamboyant pub, having glazed pillars on its frontage. The Lyric Super Cinema is shown in the background from this 1920s view, it had opened in 1897 as the Lyric Theatre, then as a cinema only between 1922 to 1925, when it re-opened as a theatre once again. Finally it was closed down in 1932 by the Liverpool Fire Brigade as a fire hazard. However, the pub survived a lot longer but was crudely demolished in the 1970s for road improvements (See page 97).*

Walton Road L4 - *This view is from 2001, photographed from Royal Street. The pub is still trading, whereas the former cinema, the Astoria closed in 1974, then became a cabaret club, and finally a bingo hall, before demolition. It was one of three former cinemas on the road, and was considered the "posh one". The other two were* the Victory, *and* the Queens *which was considered to be the "Flea Pit". The pub, the Half Way House, from time to time has been the subject of a query in local pubs over its name, with some claiming its so named as its about a five or six minute walk to both Liverpool's and Everton's ground, hence the name. Well sorry, I'm about to quash that theory! The pub was opened in the 1850s as the New Inn, and named the Half Way House by 1861, then probably re-built in 1864 (as dated) and has had the same name to date, and as the two football teams didn't exist then, that settles that!*

Palatine PH L4

The previous but one was the first building on the east side of Walton Road; this was the last building on the west side, formerly number 251, at the junction with Barlow Lane. It ceased trading in the 1930s then re-built as a shop, having various uses, but in living memory mainly remembered as Burtons Men's Outfitters (with a dance hall upstairs) and is currently open as another business. Note the children in this early view from the 1920s, no bare feet as there would have been nearer to town.

Edward Avenue L4 - *Strange this thoroughfare was even named, let alone "Avenue". The block was the full length, some 32 yards. Westward to Walton Road was Christopher Street, whereas eastward to Walton Lane was Marius Street, hard to say why it wasn't incorporated into either of the aformentioned streets. "Avenue" is normally associated with a tree lined major road, although not too far from here, off City Road is Keith Avenue, terraced houses just 94 yards long. This was originally called Keith Grove - curious indeed!*

Edward Avenue L4 - *This is Edward Avenue during demolition in 1975, photographed from the recently demolished Tate Street, and coincidentally, Tate Street was only 32 yards long.*

View L4 - *This view from 1975 is from the site of the former Edward Avenue and Tate Street, and a little further was Tetlow Street, recently demolished, with remnants of Salop Street awaiting demolition. The tall structure in the distance was a former floodlight from Goodison Park.*

Cockerell Street L4 - *Running from Walton Lane to Walton Road, this was the last block still standing when photographed in 1974; a former Mission Hall at the junction with Pugin Place, it was also in use as an Orange Lodge hall.*

Cockerell Street L4 - *In full bloom for the Coronation of Queen Elizabeth and the Duke of Edinburgh in 1953, photographed from Walton Lane, with the former corner shop known locally as "Scott's", now long demolished.*

The following four photographs show the same site, L4

Originally a private house, then named the Stanley Park Assembly Rooms. *When photographed in 1912 it stood on Walton Lane, between Langham Street and Back Langham Street. Note the shop advertising Cadbury's chocolate, and a hairdressers next door partly shown.*

This view is from 1968, the old houses on the previous view gone, and the former walled garden now built on, and was then named the Walton Lane Social Club *although it was known locally as 'Ossie Wade's' and three shops are still open.*

This view is from 1991, and more alterations have been done to the smaller section, with the name plate, Back Langham Street displayed, and Everton's ground shown on Goodison Road.

The final view is from 1998, with the original building having been demolished, and replaced by Everton's souvenir shop, which remains to date.

Claudia Street L4 - *Numerous terraced houses still stand in this part of Walton, near to Everton Football Club, and like other parts of the City, were built by Welsh builders. This particular street was demolished in the 1980s, somewhat strange only this one street was demolished in that era. Modern houses have since been built here, and this view is looking towards City Road.*

In my previous book Liverpool Our City Our Heritage *I mentioned a particular Welsh builder who left his mark on the streets of this vicinity by naming them with the first letters spelling out their name, which was* **"Owen and William Owen Elias"** *so I am repeating them for this publication as follows: They are located either side of County Road, and are still standing:* **O**xton Street, **W**inslow Street, **E**ton Street, **N**eston Street, **A**ndrew Street, **N**imrod Street. **D**ane Street, **W**ilburn Street, **I**smay Street, **L**ind Street, **L**owell Street, **I**ndex Street, **A**rnot Street, **M**akin Street, **O**lney Street, **W**eldon Street, **E**uston Street, **N**ixon Street, **E**lton Street, **L**iston Street, **I**mrie Street, **A**stor Street and **S**tuart Road.

Bedford Road L4 - *Although still trading as a furniture outlet when photographed from Euston Street in 2006, the building has since been closed and demolished. I believe a group of people tried to save it, but to no avail, and the reason for trying to save it?*

The building was a former cinema, but had the distinction of being the first purpose built cinema in Liverpool, surely that should have been reason enough to preserve it. However it's now just another piece of history that's been lost from the City, like so many others before it, and ironically in 2012 the land remains undeveloped. It had opened in December 1908, and in common with most suburban Cinemas, the late 1950s, and early 1960s was the period most cinemas closed, and this particular one, named the Bedford Hall, closed in 1959. Barely a month earlier in November 1908, the first cinema in Liverpool opened, this was the Mount Pleasant Hall, City Centre, previously having been a Wesleyan Chapel. The cinema closed in 1930. Later it became well-known as the Mardi Gras jazz club. The building was demolished in the 1970s.

Around Everton/Anfield
(1986)

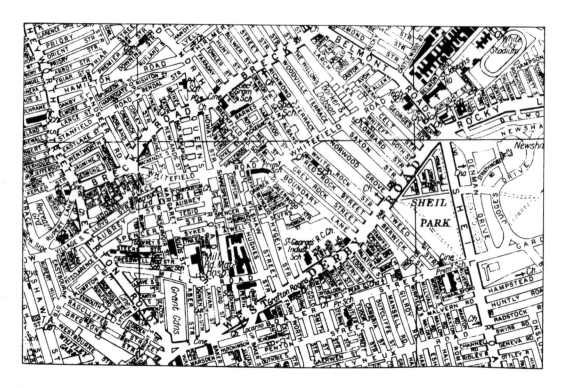

Massive and often indiscriminate housing clearance characterises the last 25 years of this district. Once again potentially fine, solid buildings were destroyed at the same time as the mean slums which richly deserved their fate. Unfortunately little is left to remind us of the interesting history of the area for few buildings have benefited from renovation. It is impossible to imagine now the rural village of Everton to which the middle classes began to move in the late eighteenth century in search of the peace of the country. High rise flats now dominate the ridge which was once covered with teeming terraced streets and when St George's Church and Our Lady Immaculate School were the tallest buildings. In more recent years policy makers have built housing estates rather than the multi storey flats which were once favoured by planners – if not the people who lived in them. In fact some tower blocks dating from the 1950s and 60s are already being demolished. We certainly do not build to last in the way our predecessors did. Two horrendous examples of modern housing are found here: the Piggeries and Radcliffe Estate. The Piggeries, which have not been honoured with a photograph, are to be found off Everton Brow. The name is given to three blocks of high rise flats built in the 1960s which now stand empty despite suggestions for both demolition and renovation. The Radcliffe Estate dating from the mid-1970s also has an undecided future. Photograph on page 102 gives a pretty clear idea of existing conditions. The estate was a planning and architectural disaster and the sooner it is demolished the better. The widespread demolition in this district has meant the break-up of the old communities but for once this is not entirely to be mourned. Religious divisions had been rife with Catholics and Protestants tending to live within specific areas. Catholics were mainly found around Scotland Road while Protestants lived in the Netherfield Road area. Serious riots and fighting had been regular occurrences on St Patrick's Day and the 12th July but as the areas were cleared and the communities dispersed from the 1950s such incidents have, fortunately, been much less frequent.

My family moved in the early 1950s to a terraced house off Blessington Road, in the nearby Anfield district where my brothers, sister, and I spent the rest of our childhood. Like many Liverpool kids, football was one of our major activities and the cobbled surface of Blessington Road was often our pitch. It seems to me now that we rarely saw a car, for the match could go on for hours disturbed only by our parents finally calling us into the house. Among the kids of the neighbourhood playing football was Kenny, younger brother of a well-known scouser, Liverpool entertainer Johnny Kennedy. Others of the old gang were Frank Darcy who later went on to play for Everton and our next door neighbour in Gurnall Street, Alan Banks, who later played for Liverpool FC (see page 145).

The once thriving district off Great Homer Street was reputed to be the busiest shopping area outside the city centre until the mid-1960s. In 1964 the new shopping precinct was being constructed when this photo was taken. So many people have been rehoused that the area is now a shadow of its former self.

The area between Great Homer Street and Everton Ridge once contained some of Liverpool's worst housing conditions as in Adelaide Place, photographed during demolition in the mid-1960s.

The Wynstay pub, at the corner of Portland Place and Roscommon Street, was derelict in 1979. Happily this fine building has been completely renovated and re-opened as a pub once more. It is now named The Cotton Picker.

The front and back of Carson Street are shown here. These 3 storey houses had no rear windows and would have had tiny backyards containing the taps for the occupants' water supply. The houses date from about 1840 and were demolished in 1964.

Thorneycliffe Street also shows early housing which must have been somewhat dark inside as only the front had windows.

Ellison Street and Luther Street showing some of Liverpool's true back-to-back houses being demolished in 1965.

These houses in Elias Street are another variation on the theme of poor terraced housing in this district. They have no back doors and the outside toilets were on the upper level between the very small yards.

The Ann Fowler Salvation Home for Women on Netherfield Road South was a well-known local landmark. This imposing listed building was originally built as a Welsh Independent chapel in 1867. It operated as a hostel until 1983 but was sadly set on fire by vandals after its closure and has had to be demolished.

Cresswell Mount was built in 1956 and was Liverpool's first completed multi-storey block. It stood at the top of St George's Hill prior to demolition in 1984.

Many of the streets on the slopes of Everton Ridge were extremely steep and had hand rails on the pavements to help pedestrians. The housing dates from the middle of the last century. Nicholson Street in 1968 is shown here.

This photograph shows the rear of the two-up, two-down houses in Patmos Street, and beyond them Our Lady Immaculate School which I attended. The school was built in the 1880s and demolished in the early 1970s (see page 120).

Cicero Terrace, running parallel to Northumberland Terrace, was typical of the average standard of housing in the area.

Northumberland Terrace at the top of the ridge would have had fine views over the city and River Mersey. These mid-Victorian houses are obviously much grander than those on the slopes below and would have been built for middle class families.

York Terrace, at the end of Northumberland Terrace, also contained some splendid dwellings. The particularly high block at the corner of Hobart Street would have had steep flights of steps to give access to the raised front doors (see page 122).

This substantial Victorian terrace stood in Everton Valley. Its grand proportions are made even more imposing by its commanding height above stone steps leading to gateways. One of these houses was the home of John Shell, a member of The Hideaways. *Tragically John, who was born in the USA, though he had always lived in Liverpool, was drafted into the US Army and was killed in Vietnam. Many will remember his funeral, with full military honours, held in Anfield in 1968.*

At the bottom of Everton Valley stood this magnificent, Victorian ornately tiled public house. The Derby Arms. *See page 85.*

The Church of Our lady Immaculate on St Domingo Road was designed by Pugin and built in 1856 as the lady chapel and chancel chapels for a proposed Roman Catholic Cathedral which was never built. The chapel instead became, and remains, the Parish church and is a listed building. The municipal tenements on the right are Sir Thomas White Gardens which were demolished in 1984.

The top of St Domingo Road is one of the highest points in Liverpool and was used as the site for a beacon from, perhaps, the thirteenth century. St George's Church, another listed building, now occupies the site. Our photograph shows nearby Beacon Lane, this large building, also by Pugin, was built in 1861 and started life as an orphanage, became a munitions factory during World War II and finally a furniture factory before it was pulled down in 1969.

The Liver pub, known as Fitzy's, was another well-known Landmark at the junction of Beacon Lane and Robson Street until it disappeared in the early 1970s. This photograph and the following four are streets on the border between Anfield and Everton. (See earlier picture on page 132)

Sleepers Hill is named after the common land that existed in the area known as 'Great & Little Sleeper'. Fortunately not all the houses off Sleepers Hill are being demolished, some are being renovated. The Stanley pub was opened in 1891 and is still open. The new housing in the background is on the site of the Liver Hotel.

Our old cobbled 'football pitch' of Blessington Road as it was in 1965. Anfield Road girls school shown in the background.

Only part of Burleigh Road South is still standing and has now been renovated. This portion and St Cuthbert's Church were demolished in 1970.

The demolition of these terraces on Towson Street should not be mourned. They were a mixture of 2 and 3 storey cellar dwellings providing poor accommodation. Anfield, home of Liverpool Football Club, can be seen in the distance.

In 1973 Desmond Street off Heyworth Street which is the continuation of St Domingo Road, was quite rightly demolished, with it went another church, St Benedicts.

Friar Street was another typical street from the 1860-80 period. It is now open grassland but new housing is scheduled for the land.

The streets off the western side of Heyworth Street were built 10-20 years earlier and were also of poor quality. This is Samuel Street and the back of Priory Road in 1966.

Druid Street and Waterhouse Street were of similar style to those shown above. The latter were especially mean with no back doors and tiny yards. The beginning of Waterhouse Street can now be traced by the street sign on the side of The Thistle public house but it only runs a few yards before petering out at the edge of the Everton Park development.

These 4 roomed houses in Sampson Street were built below street level and the road itself was never even properly surfaced. As the rear view shows, these houses also lacked back doors.

These substantial houses stood in Eastbourne Street until the large scale clearance of the 1960s. They were built for the Victorian middle classes and had elegant doorways and wrought iron balconies and railings. Fortunately, a similar terrace from 1824 on Everton Road has been saved and is being renovated.

Working class housing later surrounded Eastbourne Street. This photograph shows the rear of Village Grove situated behind the fine terrace shown on the left. The house frontages are not unusual but the back yards were completely enclosed by these high walls.

Rupert Lane was named after Prince Rupert, the Royalist general who captured Liverpool during the Civil War. He placed his headquarters on nearby Everton Brow in 1644. These three storey terraces came down in 1968.

A short distance along Everton Road stood this long landing block which nonetheless had only one entrance. This site is now landscaped.

The Radcliffe Estate off Everton Road dating from the mid-1970s is a classic example of failure by planners and architects. It was originally designed as an echo of a Cornish village; instead it was a maze of dark passages and complicated walkways.

The appropriately named Castle pub stood on the corner of Tynemouth Street and was left in splendid isolation when photographed in 1974.

Newlands Street off Breck Road was named after James Newlands, Liverpool's first borough engineer. This terrace is of 3 storey houses and as the photograph shows, the attic floors generally have no front windows, only skylights.

Another typical street was Fishguard Street shown here in 1967 when half demolished although some houses were obviously still occupied. This street was the birthplace in 1902, of Paul McCartney's father, James. The family also lived elsewhere in Everton including Solva Street and Lloyd Street both shown below. Their next home was Sir Thomas White Gardens followed by furnished rooms in Anfield where Paul was born.

Solva Street was very similar except it still retained its cobbled road probably because it was a cul-de-sac and was still unadopted in 1967.

There can be little doubt that Lloyd Street, off Everton Road, had to be demolished. The subsidence of these houses is only too evident.

Much grander houses stood in St Chrysostum Street but this did not save them. They too came down in the 1960s. How much better it would have been to renovate these elegant Victorian houses than to build the Queens Road Estate.

This housing in Back Phoebe Anne Street has to be amongst the meanest still standing in Liverpool in 1966. The houses were back-to-backs and note how few windows there are – economy housing of the early Victorian period (see page 124).

This view of the Spencer Street area shows how complete areas were cleared. Only the tower of Everton Water Works, built in 1853 by Liverpool's first Water Engineer, Thomas Duncan, now still survives.

Larch Grove stood off Larch Lea where Liverpool's 'Evertonian personality' Billy Butler grew up. The factory is Barker and Dobsons, still a thriving sweet manufacturers when photographed in 1968. Today this factory is due for demolition. Note the fine cast iron street light.

This view of Everton looking west is from 1963. Vast changes have occurred since then of course, but some structures remain, notably along the centre of the photograph. The outstanding octagonal structure was a lecture hall behind the Liverpool Collegiate School (1840/43). Who would have thought then, that the former hall would become a walled garden, with the former school now luxury apartments?

Other notable structures remaining include the fine church of St. Francis Xavier (1845/49) in the centre, which was recently renovated (and used to be the largest Catholic Parish in the country) whilst the adjoining former school, after being empty for many years, has been transformed since the late 1990s to a thriving college, named the Hope University College.

The early Georgian houses on Shaw Street (featured) still remain, and the facing Whitley Gardens also remain, whereas all the property on the bottom left has been cleared, the bottom right is a mixture of old property and 1950s built housing, all this property also demolished.

The main road running down the left, Islington (featured) has since been widened. Other notable structures are Gerard Gardens at the top/centre, demolished, and more of the walk up flats below them in this view, also demolished, they stood on Soho Street (featured).

2 Back College Street L6
On page 153 I featured this street's frontage, describing that the property had no back windows, a feature of early terraced housing. This is the rear of that street from 1966, showing the back doors into the yards, and just a blank wall having no rear windows (one step better than the true back-to-backs).

This former street's location is clearly shown on the previous page. It's immediately behind the octagonal, and named after the school, as were College Street North, South and East.

Shaw Street L6
Massive Georgian property dating c. 1830, although most are listed, they have been in a run down state for years, and more than once threatened with demolition, (some have been demolished). This view is from 2000, fortunately the bulldozer having been avoided, well almost! (see next view).

Shaw Street L6

This is the rear of a section of the previous view just 12 months later, 2001, having been completely gutted, but at least the frontage's have been saved, and so keep the character of the Georgian building, from the outside at least, and are now thoroughly renovated.

Shaw Street L6

The three previous views of Shaw Street are located on its western side, this view is from the eastern side, although not as old, they were still fine Victorian 3 storey cellar houses. This side was demolished in the 1970s, before renovation was considered for such property.

Clock PH L3

Salisbury Street now contains modern houses, shown on the aerial view (see page 107), with the old property just recently having been demolished. A pub was also built, named after a former nearby pub of the same name.

Vandalised and boarded up when photographed in 2001, also having a 'For sale' sign. However a buyer was not needed, as the pub was demolished.

Soho Street L3

Featured in Tumbling Down *page 151 this is another view of the former walk up flats that stood on Soho Street, although built in the same style as the "1930s garden flats" they weren't named, but surrounded by four thoroughfares, Soho Street, Islington, St Anne Street, and Mansfield Street, hence known locally as the four squares. This view is from 1977, during demolition.*

Gomer Street L3

The four squares, like the majority of the "garden" flats built during the 1930s often replaced older squalid property, and this is one example, formerly number 4 court in Gomer Street (demolished) in this vicinity, photographed in 1927.

The area around the four squares was largely a Catholic area in the 1960s and earlier, and such was the way the population grew from the 19th Century. Just half a mile or so further north was largely an Orange Lodge area. The following view shows a tradition all but finished now, a May procession of girls from St Mary of the Angels in 1963 (see next page).

View L3 - *They would leave from the back gate of the Friary School, Bute Street, then along Fox Street, Richmond Row, St Anne Street, Queen Anne Street, through the four squares, into Soho Street, then up Everton Brow to Watmough Street, then down Bute Street, into Fox Street, then into the Church for the Crowning.*

Fox Street L3 - *This view from 1992 shows the former church, beyond an old block that had been derelict for years, and the corner section was a PH many years ago, the Richmond Arms, (featured in* A Pub On Every Corner Volume 4*) the block has since been demolished, leaving the former church in isolation.*

St Anne Street L3 - *A remnant from when St Anne Street was the home to the wealthy residents of the town in the early 19th century, before they fled to pastures new as the town expanded. This Georgian block at the junction of St Anne Street and Springfield still standing when photographed in 1999 and although listed, would soon fall victim to the bulldozer, together with the adjoining pub, the Wellington. A modern fire station now stands on this site.*

Sheriff Street L5 - *High rise flats loom in the background on Netherfield Road South when this was photographed in 1964, many of the old streets of the vicinity having been demolished, or in the process of, at the time. The side elevation was Sheriff Street, 3 roomed houses, although having narrow outriggers, with the bricked up door on the right being a house on Beresford Street.*

Conway Street L5
The bulldozer busy as Conway Street, off Netherfield Road North is about to be obliterated, together with the surrounding streets in the 1960s; note St George's Church looming in the background.

Netherfield Road North L5
Further north, and the old houses off the western side of Netherfield Road North are also about to be obliterated when photographed in 1967 and a new tower block, under construction, is shown in the background.

Ellison Street/Luther Street L5

This view from 1965, the centre block, Luther Street was a true back-to-back block, very rare by the 1960s, which means no entry between the houses of Ellison Street, so just three roomed houses on Ellison Street, and two roomed houses on Luther Street. My former school, Our Lady Immaculate, is shown in the background, higher up on the left on the Everton ridge (see page 120).

Seven Stars P H L5

By the 1970s most of the old streets between Netherfield Road North and Great Homer Street had been obliterated, one such street being Gordon Street, and this view from 1972 is of a new pub in the former street, together with new housing in the vicinity. Since then it's been all change again, the pub gone, new housing of the time gone, and modern housing built once again in the vicinity (see page 116).

Coronation Court L9 - *This view of the highrise flats is from Lower Lane on the Sparrow Hall Estate, Fazakerley, photographed in 2002 during demolition. Construction started in 1953, the year of the queen's coronation, hence the name.*

The greatest housing mistake since the war? This depends on one's point of view of course, but as described in the "Dock" section, the chronic shortage of housing after the war did need drastic action, and such property did fill the gap. The trouble was, far too many were constructed, particularly here in Everton. Of course many other areas both in Liverpool and the outskirts also had them, such as Croxteth, Kirkby, Huyton, Childwall, Netherley, Halewood and Sefton Park.

By the late 1960s over 100 were standing, and these "communities in the sky" eventually became similar to housing in general, in that some remained popular, others became undesirable, and this type of property also began to tumble down. It was the 1970s and 1980s that the rot set in, probably the most well documented were the infamous "Piggeries" the nickname given to Crosby, Canterbury and Haigh Heights in William Henry Street, which literally became "slums in the sky" and are documented in "Liverpool Our City Our Heritage".

Such was the unpopularity of the high rise flats, during the 1980s two of them, Brynford and Milburn Heights, in Conway Street, were actually sold for peanuts! Apparently something like 10p, or 20p a flat; it later emerged that asylum seekers were living in them in poverty.

They were sold off again to a property group in 2001, and here's a sting in the tail, within two years they were transformed into affordable executive apartments, and in May 2003, the first 50 were sold, snapped up in a matter of hours!

An amazing transformation of abandoned flats, then tenanted by asylum seekers, to desirable apartments. So what was the first constructed? The photo above and the top photograph on the following page were the first constructed in Liverpool, one built first, one tenanted first, so take your pick!!

Cresswell Mount L5

Photographed during demolition in 1984, located in Everton Terrace, although Coronation Court was the first to commence, for various reasons. It wasn't finished on time, so this block, started in 1954, and officially opened in 1956 became the first to be completed and tenanted. It was named after Jack Cresswell, a former deputy chairman of the housing committee.

View L5

Photographed from Great Homer Street, this view from 1969 shows the old street's obliterated as far as Netherfield Road North, St George's Church looming in the background, and three high rise flats on Netherfield Road North. They were Edinburgh Tower, Seacombe Tower, and Ellison Tower, named after three of the former streets of the vicinity.

Thomaston Street area L5

The same three blocks shown on this view from 2000, from the Thomaston Street area, with another block, Corinth Tower on the left. The 1970s jerry built housing shown during demolition after barely 30 years, and brand new houses already built, such as the bungalow partly shown on the left. Before the 1970s houses were built, Thomaston Street was just one of numerous terraced streets that existed between Netherfield Road North and Great Homer Street.

View L5

Three years after the last view in 2003, the high rise flats shown previously are now undergoing demolition themselves, this picture showing the middle block almost demolished.

Netherfield Road North L5

This area was largely Orange Lodge territory, and this former PH, the King Edward, was listed numbers 1/3, the huge St George's Heights looming in the background.

When photographed in 1973, the side view shows graffiti, LOL (Loyal Orange Lodge) and UVF (Ulster Volunteer Force) relating to the former troubles in Ireland. The road is still the meeting point for the Orange Lodge Order every July 12th when they gather for their traditional day out to Southport.

Many years ago a special licence enabled the pubs to open earlier on the 12th enabling a few pints to be had before marching to town, and the pubs would be very busy until they began their march. Over the last few years this tradition has now gone and it's not that they've all suddenly become teetotal, it's simply that no more pubs remain on the road (18 pre-war - see next view).

St George's Heights - *This view shows the former huge block undergoing demolition in 2000, the comparatively modern pub, the Tugboat, not included in the previous list of course, and it has been closed for a number of years to date.*

Netherfield Road North L5 - *This view from 1968 features the John Bagot Ear Nose and Throat Hospital, formerly located on the east side of the road between Havelock Street, and Mitford Street. It had opened in 1888 as the "City Hospital for infectious diseases" one of two at the time, the other was opened in Grafton Street, in the south end of the City. The hospital was demolished in the 1970s, and a small housing development was constructed, and aptly named John Bagot Close. Part of the original wall still stands, and on the extreme right partly shown is more "religious graffiti" common in the area at the time.*

Torr Street L5 - *Formerly running from Netherfield Road north to St Domingo Road when the old houses were standing, featuring large 1950s built four storey houses awaiting demolition when photographed in 1991, with the street since re-aligned when more modern houses were built.*

Devonshire Place L5 - *Devonshire Place (realigned) is off the eastern side of Netherfield Road North, adjacent to the previous street. This view from 2002, shows another high rise in the last stages of demolition, the block was named Rock View, the 1950s built maisonettes on the left also since demolished.*

Our Lady Immaculate RC School - *This view of the old "dungeon on the Hill" as it was fondly known, and in the 1960s it was one of only two structures that could be seen from the River Mersey, towering over the terraced property. The other is St George's Church (1812-1814) on the top of the Everton ridge, which contains the earliest example of the use of prefabricated cast iron sections in the vaults, columns, and ribs of the church, by the renowned architect Thomas Rickman, and since the demise of tower blocks, the church still stands proudly on the Everton ridge.*

This view shows the rear of houses on York Terrace on the left, 253 yards long, and Seville Street, 74 yards long, on the right, after the frontage on Netherfield Road North had been demolished, but doesn't really show how steep it was (see next view) the entry in the middle holds fond memories from my school days, as when playing football in the school yard, when the ball went over the wall someone (usually who ever owned the ball) had to run down the entry, across the main road, then nearly as far as Great Homer Street to get the ball back! Happy days! (a separate view of the school is shown on page 96).

Hapton Street L5 - *Photographed in 2008, after the old property had been demolished, originally 57 yards long, and was next to Seville Street, demolished, and still remains as a thoroughfare. A former Methodist Mission is at the corner of Netherfield Road North, and behind it stood a former cinema, the Popular. Over 100 cinemas once existed in the City, and this one closed in 1956, and from this date through to the 1960s saw numerous closures as more and more families obtained televisions.*

The former Pop, as it was known, was also a magnet for us kids as a play area when derelict, a dangerous place, but not to us kids, no health and safety then! Although only photographed in 2008, it's all since been demolished, the wall in the centre was the only remnant left of the former cinema.

Hapton Street L5 - *This view from Netherfield Road North is from 2002, with Hapton Street on the right, and another example of comparative modern housing at this junction that has since been demolished.*

York Terrace L5 - *Higher up the ridge from the smaller houses shown on the school photograph, stood much larger former merchants' houses, shown here in 1966 during demolition, at the junction with the former Hobart Street, (separate views shown on page 97).*

Daniel Street L5 - *Formerly located off Northumberland Terrace on the ridge, one side having been demolished, and the other awaiting the same fate when photographed in 1969.*

Willis Square L5 - *This tiny street was only 14 yards long, located off Northumberland Terrace at the summit of the Everton ridge, near St George's Church. An old warehouse awaiting demolition looms in the background when photographed in 1965.*

Jefferson Street L5 - *This was one of the former teeming streets off the western side of Heyworth Street, formerly running down to Druid Street, from which corner the photograph was taken, and reduced to just a shell when photographed during demolition in 1967; now part of Everton Park.*

Copeland Street L5
This view showing the rear of Copeland Street, a little north of the previous view, having very small yards between the outriggers, with the recently built St George's Heights in the background when photographed in 1966. Just out of view to the left the steep hill drops dramatically as shown in the next view.

Copeland Street L5
This view showing the derelict state of the rear of the houses as the street dramatically drops down. Note that the bottom half of the street didn't have out-riggers, just small yards; had they stood much longer, they would have tumbled down themselves!

Stonewall Street L5 - *Adjoining the previous street, these appear to be fine three storey terraced houses, soon to be demolished, and once again, shows how the street rapidly descends down to Everton Terrace.*

Mill Road L6 - *Early terraced houses on Mill Road, off the eastern side of Everton Road when photographed in 1966. Note the "stable" in the middle of the block; it would most probably have been used as a "cow shed" years ago.*

Mill Road L6 - *A close up of two adjoining doors of the old housing in Mill Road, the rubble on the right of the previous view was the site of these two houses, and was photographed just before demolition in 1966. Mill Road has since been realigned, and now contains modern housing.*

Back Phoebe Anne Street L6 - *Very poor back-to-back housing still standing in the 1960s, (a different view is on page 105) looking more like barns rather than houses, and the "alley" was 56 yards long, and located off Mill Road when photographed in 1966.*

Breck Road L5 - *This major road runs westward from Everton Road/Heyworth Street to Oakfield Road/Belmont Road and then continues as Breck Road Anfield. North of the road is L5, and south L6, beyond Breckfield Road North/Breckfield Road South westward. Many of the three storey blocks, and terraced streets still remain on Breck Road, whereas eastward they have all been cleared. This was one of those blocks, at the junction of Baines Place in the 1960s, long since replaced by landscaping and housing.*

Harriet Terrace L6 - *Before demolition in the 1960s, Queens Road, off Breck Road, consisted mainly of large three storey Victorian houses. This particular block of two storey cellar houses was actually on Queens Road, and was probably built in either the 1840s or 1850s, before the larger houses were constructed.*

Lloyd Street L6

Located off the eastern side of Everton Road, this view is from 1967 as the street was undergoing demolition, the Everton waterworks (reservoir) in the background.

This was one of three streets that Paul McCartney's parents, Jim and Mary, lived in. The other two were Solva Street and Fishguard Street, all three being in close proximity. The latter two streets both featured together with a different view of Lloyd Street (see page 104).

I mistakenly said in the original publication that "their next home was in Sir Thomas White Gardens followed by furnished rooms in Anfield where Paul was born". In fact it was the other way around. Paul did indeed live in furnished rooms in Sunbury Road, Anfield, after his birth in Walton Hospital 1942. The family did then move to a flat in Sir Thomas White Gardens, in conjunction with his mother's job as a midwife. (See Beacon Lane, page 129).

Margaret Street L6

Featuring the reservoir in the previous view from another angle, also from the 1960s as a thin layer of snow lies on the ground. The pub at the end of Margaret Street was at the junction of Whitefield Road, and Brunel Street, and was aptly named the Reservoir Vaults (featured in Volume Four, A Pub On Every Corner).

Newlands Walk L6 - *Three decades after the previous two views, and the reservoir shown once again, only this time surrounded by 1970s built houses awaiting demolition when photographed in 1991. This vicinity was known as the Queens Road Estate, and has since been replaced with better quality housing.*

Pickering Street / Rothwell Street L6
Formerly located off Breckfield Road South, this terraced block on Pickering Street, photographed in the 1960s, was unusual in being built of stone, unlike the majority of terraced houses which were built with brick. Also note the unusually large gas lamp. The site of these streets is now part of a car park for a shopping mall.

The following two were located south of West Derby Road

Rockwood Street/Vivian Street area L6
Amongst a cluster of terraced streets south of West Derby Road during demolition in the 1970s, all since replaced with modern housing. The spire in the centre back ground was Emmanuel Church, consecrated in 1867, and was at the junction of West Derby Road, and Boaler Street.

Guthrie Street L6
Also in this vicinity, and formerly located off Upper Baker Street, like the latter, demolished in the 1970s.

Butler Terrace L6
Formerly situated between Butler Street and Sterne Street, off Boaler Street, one of two terraces, the other was Sterne Terrace, and were both 40 feet in length.

I am now returning to the Beacon Lane vicinity

Beacon Lane L5

This view of Beacon Lane from the early 1960s looking northward, was taken outside the Beacon Light PH, on the right, formerly listed number 80/82, at the junction of Wye Street, one of 5 pubs in Beacon Lane (see Liver Hotel). Beyond the terraced houses the end of the Alexandra PH can partly be seen, (featured) and on the left was Sir Thomas White Gardens. (featured).

A stairwell can be seen jutting out on the flats, immediately adjacent to it on the ground floor was where Paul McCartney lived as a youngster for a couple of years. A friend of mine, Alex Marr, recalls the following...

"My late mother, Alice, lived by the Alexandra Pub right facing the flat where Mary (Paul's and Michael's mother) lived, at No.76. She was popular in the area as she was the local midwife, but not only for the flats, but the surrounding streets also. A woman named Cathy lived above Mary on the first landing, and she would often "baby sit" the boys when Mary was called out at night. Mary did work long hours at times, and although she got on well with the women, I don't think she particularly liked the area, and wanted a better environment to bring up her children, and so she left after about two years, and moved to Speke in south Liverpool."

Sir Thomas White Gardens L5 - *This section of the former walk up flats was photographed from Penrose Street in 1985 (see next view) shortly before demolition, the old wall shown on the right still remaining after the flats were demolished. This is a remnant from the former St Domingo House, later St Edward's College, that stood here before the flats were built in the 1930s. They were named after Sir Thomas White, a former leader of the City's Conservative Party, who died in 1938.*

I walked through these former flats daily with my brothers, sister, and friends when at school, and occasionally we would encounter sectarian trouble, not that we'd even heard of the word then, just the Orange and the Green to us, and our school was in an Orange area anyway, although Catholics also lived here. Religion didn't come into another memory of the flats, and that was the game of football in the big square, it was amazing, no one ever knew how many a side were playing, it could have been anything up to 30 odd each team, or even more, and the score would be as high, no one ever got it quite right, far too many goals!

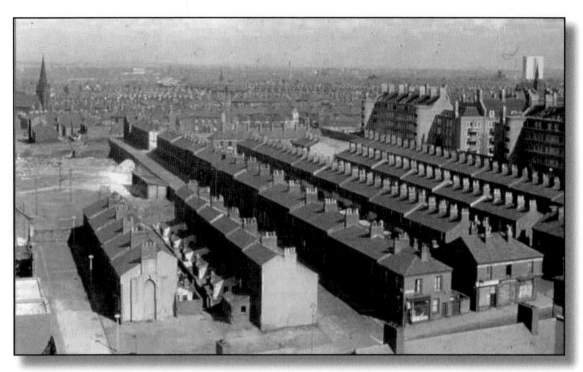

View L5 - *This view looking east across St Domingo Road shows Sir Thomas White Gardens on the right from the late 1960s, the streets shown prior to demolition from the flats were Penrose Street, Carmel Street, Calder Street, and Hodder Street, and beyond Hodder Street on the left is a former quarry, then Corporation yard, and the church on the extreme left was St Cuthberts, at the junction of Robson Street and Burleigh Road South.*

Our Lady Immaculate Church L5 - *Formerly located on St Domingo Road, facing York Terrace, on page 98. I wrote the following:* ***"The church of Our Lady Immaculate on St Domingo Road was designed by Pugin and built in 1856 as the lady chapel and chancel chapels for a proposed Roman Catholic cathedral, which was never built, the chapel instead became, and remains, the parish church and is a listed building".***

Sadly, listed status did not save the church, as this view shows, photographed just four years later during demolition in 1990.

Alexandra P H L5

This is the pub mentioned in the Beacon Lane view, formerly listed number 134 Beacon Lane, at the junction of Breckfield Road North, shown on the left, and was photographed looking southward, towards the Beacon Light in 1969.

Liver Hotel L5

This view from 1967 was the Liver Hotel, formerly 129 Robson Street and 200 Beacon Lane, the houses on the left (Robson Street) remain, whilst the church, St Cuthbert's (shown on the last but three view) has been demolished, so too the pub, and former houses of Beacon Lane, and the vicinity around the former Beacon Lane has since been re-built as the Grizedale estate.

The other two pubs on Beacon Lane were the Brighton Hotel, formerly listed number 178, and since demolished, and surprisingly, the fifth pub actually still survives in Beacon Lane, although not recognizable as such with all the changes. It's the Stanley Hotel, now listed just 70 Walton Breck Road, and before the Grizedale estate was built, it was listed number 70, and 199 Beacon Lane. (a later view is on page 98) and the five pubs in Beacon Lane are all featured in A Pub On Every Corner, Volume 4*).*

Lansdowne Place L5 - *As featured throughout this publication, numerous "modern" houses have been destroyed. These houses, off Mere Lane, were only tenanted in 1980/81, yet less than 25 years later, as this view from 2003 shows, about to be demolished.*

Breckfield Road North L5

A large Methodist Chapel dominates this view from the 1960s, which was at the junction of St Domingo Vale, and it was here that Everton Football Club had its roots, back in the 1870s. In those days local cricket and football teams were associated with churchs and chapels. A cricket team was established shortly after Stanley Park opened in 1870 by members of this chapel (then named as the New Connexion Chapel) and they played in the new park, cricket in the summer, and football in the winter, and in 1878 they added a "St Domingo Football Club" officially to their Cricket Club.

The following year, 1879, it was decided to change the name of the Football Club to the district they belonged, and so Everton Football Club was established. During the 1880s football came on in leaps and bounds, particularly when professionalism was adopted into the game, and in 1888 arguably the most important event in the history of professional football transpired. The football league was established, and twelve teams were chosen for the inauguration, with Everton amongst them, and since then to date, Everton have played in the top tier more times than any other football club in the country, having played only four seasons in the second tier.

A plaque in the structure that replaced the Chapel, Liberton Court, records Everton's greatest ever player as follows:

THIS PLAQUE WAS UNVEILED BY
MR PHILIP CARTER CBE
CHAIRMAN OF EVERTON FOOTBALL CLUB ON 5th MAY 1988
IN HONOUR OF THE 60th ANNIVERSARY OF THE 60th GOAL SCORED BY
WILLIAM RALPH "DIXIE" DEAN IN 1928

That goal, in the 1927/28 season was an unsurpassable League record, scoring 60 in only 39 games, and on the day Everton clinched the League title, he actually scored 100 goals overall that season, just two of "Dixie's" many records during his career.

Breckfield Road North L5 - *Not too far from the previous view, on the opposite side of the road stood another church, St Saviour's, at the junction of Downing Street, a block of shops next to it, and on the other corner a pub, the Rutland, at the junction of Rutland Street, all now long vanished.*

St Saviour's L5 - *Showing the huge church undergoing demolition in 1988. It had been consecrated exactly 120 years earlier, in 1868, and so like the latter, and in fact as shown throughout this publication, sadly, many of the City's former churchs have been lost over the years.*

Lorraine Street School L5
Formerly located off Breckfield Road North, and photographed in 2000 during demolition, the site now part of a recently built school, named the North Liverpool Academy School.

Robson Street L5
A three storey block at the junction of Vienna Street in the course of demolition when photographed in 1980, with the pub at the other junction soon to follow the same fate. I frequented this pub, named the Sefton, before its closure. It was a typical small but very busy local, and was one of the last to still use the old "bell" service from a tiny back parlour, and also still had the toilet in the back yard!

Robson Street/Granton Road L5 - *This view, higher up on the same side as the previous view, is only from 2006, and in fact the café adjoining the empty Granton PH was still open. With the exception of the ornate lamp, all the property in this view has since been demolished.*

Granton Road L5 - *This view is from 2007, half way down the road, and another local about to bite the dust together with the houses. Listed number 93, the Salisbury, which was known for years as the "little Sali" to distinguish it from a pub of the same name on the nearby Walton Breck Road.*

Burleigh Road South L5 - *Sadly, with the mass demolition over the years of both old and new properties, fine housing stock also still continues to tumble down. This is a good example, well built large Victorian cellar/attic houses that stood on Burleigh Road South, off Walton Breck Road. In fact they had actually been renovated, yet these fine houses were almost all empty when photographed in 2000.*

2nd view L5 - *Here is the same block just a year later, 2001, and as shown photographed during demolition. Such demolition does create controversy, local people would often say what would such houses be worth in London? Academic of course, this is Liverpool, and such property is not appreciated here, as in London. This road used to continue across Robson Street through what is now the Grizedale estate, and that section is featured on page 99.*

Varthen Street L5 - *This shows the street empty and awaiting demolition in 2010, one of a cluster of seven known as the "V" Streets of the vicinity, off Walton Breck Road. It was 92 yards long, and at the top is a former school (next view) demolition only started in the last decade of these streets, after years of uncertainty for the residents. The others were, Venmore Street, 400 yards long, (see Park PH) partly demolished, Vienna Street, 354 yards long, partly demolished, Venice Street, 287 yards long,(featured) partly demolished, and three shorter streets, Vyrnwy Street, 95 yards long, demolished, Vanguard Street, 50 yards long, demolished, and Viceroy Street, 43 yards long, demolished; note the Welsh named connection.*

Venice Street School L5
Showing the ongoing demolition of the former Venice Street School and vicinity when photographed in 2010, and has since been completely demolished.

Venice Street L5 - *Typical two-up two-down terraced houses, photographed from Vyrnwy Street, as they await their fate when boarded up in 2010.*

Walton Breck Road L4 - *A bus in the distance, and the old tram lines still in evidence in this 1950s view of Walton Breck Road. The wall on the right fronting the old kop end of LFC, now long vanished, whilst the adjoining pub, advertising "Walker's Falstaff Ale", the Albert, still remains, listed 185 Walton Breck Road. The block on the extreme left was demolished in the early 1960s, and replaced by a church, Holy Trinity, the pub at the other junction of Towson Street, the Park Hotel, also remains open, listed 194 Walton Breck Road and 183 Towson Street, displaying the old "Bents" sign over the door. The next two photographs are modern views of the two pubs.*

Walton Breck Road L4

The Albert PH, is featured in this view from 2007, looking in the opposite direction from the previous view, it's the building nearest to Liverpool's Football Ground, all the other property from Gilman Street since demolished.

Park PH L5 - *This is the Park Hotel in 2011, the adjoining property having been demolished, and the houses of Venmore Street empty and awaiting their fate, one side having recently been cleared. The pub is the oldest on the road, as despite displaying a date of 1888, a pub of the same name was listed on this site in the 1850s, it was most probably rebuilt in 1888.*

The streets on the opposite side of Walton Breck Road are in Anfield, L4, and demolition has been going on since 2006. At the time of writing Lake Street, Tinsley Street, and half of Gilman Street have been demolished. The remainder, from Gilman Street to Pulford Street, currently contain many boarded up houses, and in March 2012, it was revealed, after years of uncertainty, that they will be demolished (that's the current situation, it remains to be seen with ever changing policies if demolition does occur).

Kemlyn Road L4

Before proceeding to the vicinity north west of the ground, I am going back two decades to the opposite side of the ground, the former Kemlyn Road. This view is from 1991, and shows the last house in Kemlyn Road during demolition, and the end of a long saga. Liverpool Football Club had acquired the land for a car park extension, and the houses were demolished in the 1980s, well, most of them, the last one still standing belonged to two elderly sisters who refused to move. This situation dragged on for some years, until they finally left, and as shown, demolition finally occurred in 1991.

The left shows the turnstiles of what remained of the former wall of the ground, and the block on the right, displaying Walton Breck Road was demolished some years later, the mansion houses centre top, on Anfield Road, were demolished during the "noughties" and Kemlyn Road now no longer exists. (see Liverpool Football Ground).

Lake Street L4
This street, the first to go, was photographed only literally seconds before the block, only a matter of yards from Liverpool's Football Ground, was about to bite the dust, in 2006, and its site is now a car park, with the rear of the Albert PH partly shown. Further along towards Gilman Street is currently landscaped.

Rockfield Road L4

I mentioned in the Scotland Road section anti-social behaviour and how it can destroy communities, and this road is a prime example. Prior to the 1990s it was just an ordinary road of fine Victorian houses, like so many others in the City, that is until the 1990s, when rogue landlords acquired some of the houses, and often sub-let them, and it deteriorated rapidly. This in turn led to anti-social behaviour, fires became common place, and as people moved out, more fires, and vandalism, with many houses left in a ruinous state. In fact it became that bad, some taxi drivers wouldn't even drive into the road, and the nickname of "Beirut" was soon given to it.

From about six or seven years ago it did slowly improve, as housing associations began to acquire the vacant properties, but so too did private landlords, and the rogue ones still continue to place "problem families" in the area, and although anti-social behaviour still continues, the police do take it more seriously than a decade ago. Most of the empty houses are now tinned up properly, with fires now rare, unlike the late 1990s, and early into the new millennium, when they were frequent. Tancred Road, off Rockfield, has since been refurbished, whereas Coningsby Road, and Sybil Road, also off Rockfield, have had some improvements, and work is still ongoing in the immediate vicinity, albeit piecemeal.

Yet having said that, we're now into the second decade of the 21st century, and the actual road is still a disgrace, far too many boarded up houses, and I'm going to recall an incident that happened in 2002. Liverpool were at home on a Saturday afternoon and I was on the step, with my late wife, Jean, who was cleaning the brass on the front door, when a Japanese couple had wandered into the road on the way to the match, and quite innocently, and politely, asked her *"Is this a war zone?"*.

Fast forward to March 4th 2010, and a two page spread in the *Liverpool Echo* about Anfield, or to be more precise, this part of Anfield, suffice to record one paragraph from Walton MP, Peter Kilfoyle, as follows:

"It needs a total sweep through, to get it all done, particularly Rockfield Road. We have a lot of people coming here from overseas and what must they think about the area? It must give a very bad impression".

Then the following month, on the 26th also in the *Liverpool Echo*, the following was part of an article by Warren Bradley, council leader, concerning the City:

"We turned the streets into war zones"

March 2012, and the latest plans from the council indicate the houses are staying up, albeit with some being demolished, so after some 15 or 16 years it now appears there's light at the end of the tunnel, but when? Hopefully sooner, rather than later, it should be a road fit to live in, in 2013, and beyond.

Rockfield Road L4

As stated, fires were common place, not just at night, but also during the day. This view from 2000 was taken as I had just pulled up in a car, and flames were shooting out of a window of a house facing the end of the road, in Lothair Road.

Rockfield Road L4

Showing a portion of the road vandalised and with graffiti when photographed in 2002. This was at the height of the road's troubles. Fortunately it is not as bad now as just stated, in the previous but one paragraph (see page 242).

Blessington Road L4

As I mentioned in the Kirkdale section, many of the main road blocks of former shops have been swept away since the introduction of supermarkets, and out of town shopping malls, but many of the minor roads, such as this one also contained shops. It's 227 yards in length, and in the 1960s contained 30 shops, and 2012? Just one, an off-licence, at the junction with Sleepers Hill which wasn't trading in the 1960 list (see next page). I featured the road on page 99 describing it as "our old cobbled football pitch" in 1965. This view, taken from outside the King Harry PH is from 1966.

The following shops were trading in 1960

Blessington Road L4

2/4 Liverpool Co-operative Society Ltd

6 Confectioner

8 Hairdresser

10 Cleaners and Dyers

12 Pet Food Dealer

22 General Dealer

24 Shopkeeper

34 Electrician

38 Chandlers

40 Butchers

42 Draper

44a Draper

46 Milliner

48 Sub Post Office

50 Shopkeeper

56 Tea Dealer and Storeroom

58 Handicraft Supplies Dealer

60 Confectioner

62 Greengrocer

3a Butchers

27 Launderers

29 Chandlers

31 Tobacconist

33 Fried Fish Dealer

35 Greengrocer

37 Shopkeeper

39 Confectioner

47 Radio Engineers

49 Shopkeeper

53 Tobacconist

Although many traded as the same business for years, others changed. For example, I can recall number 34, at the other end of the block where I lived was an old-fashioned Fish Shop; having the fish displayed on slanting marble slabs out in the open, and the premises were also in use as one of the earliest mini-cab offices in Liverpool.

Gurnall Street L4

This is one of the streets off Blessington Road, my old street, and but for the old Thames Trader Lorry, it could have been photographed today, not when I took it in 1967, well almost. There was no boarded up houses back then, and there's a story regarding the lorry as follows...

It was my next door neighbour, Harry Banks, who drove it, belonging to the firm, LBM (Liverpool Building Material) which was formerly located in Mere Lane. Harry had two sons, and two daughters. I worked with one, Harry, in the old fruit market in Queen Square, and the docks, whereas Alan, a plumber, went on to become a professional footballer. He played for Liverpool from 1958 - 1961, and although at the club for three years, he only made 8 first team appearances, yet scoring a creditable 6 goals. My brothers and I would play footie in the street with both Alan and Harry when we were kids.

It was the signing of Ian St John that prompted Alan to move on from playing for Liverpool, and he played for a number of teams in the lower divisions, Cambridge City, Exeter City, Plymouth Argyle, and Poole Town. Although Exeter City was his main club, having two stints from 1963 - 1966 and 1967 - 1973, in the two stints he scored 101 senior goals from 258 appearances, and in a survey published by the Professional Footballers' Association in December 2007, Alan Banks was listed as the all-time favourite player amongst Exeter City fans. In Alan's senior career he played 285 games, scoring 112 goals.

Blessington Road/Gurnall Street L4

This view from 2009 is the opposite corner from the previous view, with the former corner shop and house in Gurnall Street having been demolished, and currently is the only demolition to occur in the vicinity except for the previously mentioned streets adjacent to the ground, yet like the near-by Rockfield Road, the Blessington Road vicinity also began a gradual decline over the years, particularly since the new millennium, and in line with the shop closures.

The last but one to close was a sweet shop, No. 60, facing the King Harry Pub, (a greengrocers on the 1960 list) and this was forced to close after numerous break-ins, and acts of vandalism. Yet, also like Rockfield Road, long awaited plans for regeneration were finally approved in March 2012, and work has started. It involves both demolition and regeneration, and will be known as the "Anfield Village" so hopefully, in the near future, it should become a desirable place to live once again, shouldn't it?

Liverpool Football Club L4

Two views of fine Victorian Villas on Anfield Road, sadly derelict when photographed in 2002, so why under Liverpool Football Club?

Before giving a reason I'll mention the actual Football Ground; its location is in the midst of the previous mentioned streets, and blamed by many for the depravation and run down state of the vicinity, which is nonsense of course. The club is a "Business" that's been here for 120 years, and the houses even longer. The run down state is down to the "powers that be" here in Liverpool over the last couple of decades, and as featured throughout this publication. Similar situations have been happening in all the inner-city areas for decades. Had the new Ground been built in the last decade as planned, it may well have accelerated regeneration, which as I've described, has finally started. So why feature two villas? The reason is that after numerous legal wrangles during the last decade, the club was finally given permission to build a new Ground in Stanley Park, in 2005, after first announcing the scheme in 2000. Part of the massive scheme was renovation of Stanley Park (completed, including the demolition of Vernon Sangster sports centre) demolition on Priory Road (completed) and demolition of fine mansion houses on Anfield Road, including the two featured (completed). Since then, circumstances have completely changed. Briefly, new American owners took over, a disaster, now mainly remembered when co-owner, George Gillett uttered the following infamous words regarding the new stadium "THE SHOVEL NEEDS TO BE IN THE GROUND IN THE NEXT 60 DAYS OR SO" in 2007. This never happened as the new American owner, John W Henry (Fenway Sports Group), put the ground on the back burner. Then late in 2010 they said information of the new Ground would be forthcoming, with an option to rebuild the current Ground, and if that was to happen, the houses in the two views, amongst others (see Kemlyn Road) would have been demolished for nothing, hence the reason for featuring them. When permission was given in 2005, the deal included a 999 year lease for the new Ground, and the time scale for it to go ahead ran out in June 2011, and with all the uncertainty the club was given a three month's extension. That passed, and nothing was forthcoming in 2012 until just before this book was going for publication, and it verifies the previous paragraph as being correct, as it was announced on 15th October that the current Ground would be redeveloped, therefore when going to print I can only make one more point after some 12 years of the Ground saga, and that is, SURELY THIS CAN'T BE ANOTHER FALSE DAWN, CAN IT?

Tram L4

A form of transport gradually fading from memory, a former tram. This was route No. 19a, having just left Sleepers Hill into Anfield Road, and about to turn right into Walton Lane en route to Kirkby when photographed in the 1950s. The church alongside the tram was a former Welsh Methodist Chapel, since demolished and replaced by housing. The former school on the other side of Walton Lane was also demolished, yet the small block of terraced houses partly shown alongside the chapel on Anfield Road, still remain.

Stanley Park L4

Three children in a snow covered Stanley Park from the early 1960s and they are Colin and Paul Prior, and their sister, Maureen. The location is almost parallel to the previous view, about 50 yards away. The school on the left, (partly shown on the last view) and terraced street on the right are now long gone, yet the former Stanley Park Church in the centre still remains to date.

From Islington to Edge Hill
(1986)

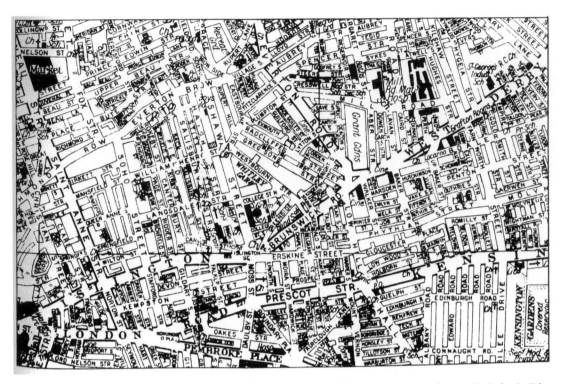

Islington runs east from the grand suite of municipal buildings that stands on St John's Plateau overlooking the city. Today, sadly, the grandeur of Liverpool ends where Islington begins. The complete frontage of the street has disappeared in the path of a new road scheme, though it must be admitted that many of the buildings had already fallen into disrepair.

The whole area around Islington has been in a state of flux for some years now. The prime causes have been twofold; the building of the new Royal Liverpool Hospital complex which swallowed large amounts of land, and major road building schemes have cut huge swathes through the district. These were connected with the completion of the Wallasey tunnel under the Mersey and the need to improve commuter routes to the city. Large numbers of houses have been cleared and shops in the area now struggle for survival. Most recent building has been for industrial and commercial uses in an attempt to bring work back to the area. It is ironic that in the late eighteenth and early nineteenth century this locality was a well off, middle class area. St Anne Street named after the church which stood there, even had genteel sports facilities: an archery range, a bowling green and a tennis court. However, the city was then expanding so rapidly that all this would have been swallowed up soon after the turn of the century by working class housing such as courts and low quality terraces. From later periods this area also had several interesting examples of landing blocks and some are shown on the following page.

In Edge Hill part of the old village centre fortunately still stands around Mount Vernon Road and Holland Place and some buildings are now being renovated. The hill on which stood the Lybro factory is one of the highest points in South Lancashire and in 1886 was the site for the Liverpool Shipperies Exhibition. For this large commercial exhibition a replica of the Eddystone lighthouse, over 130 feet high, was erected. The light could be seen for 40 miles and the view from the top must have been magnificent. There is still a pub in Durning Road called the Shipperies which commemorates this exhibition but nothing else remains.

St Anne Street police station now stands on the site of this 'landing' block. This is a relatively late example dating from just before the First World War.

This large tenement block was built in 1923 when the old court dwellings were being cleared. It stood on Holly Street off St Anne Street.

Close to Mansfield Street stands a building erected for a carriage hire business in 1876. It still carries an inscription, not showing here, which advertises 'Wedding Equipages, Broughams, Phaetons, Private Omnibuses, Waggonettes and Funeral Carriages and all other requisites'.

It also claims 'Appointments of a Superior Description'. Presumably this was the home of the forerunner of today's car hire business.

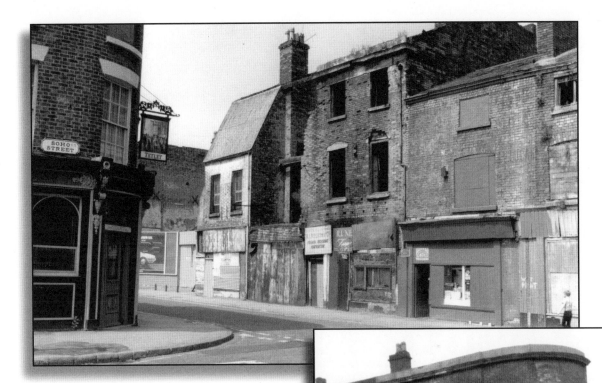

Richmond Row running into Fox Street is the site of this dilapidated hotchpotch of buildings which is surprisingly still standing at the time of writing. It is obviously many years since the upper storeys were used. Richmond Row was the original route between Everton and the city centre.

The Soho Street area now seems to have an air of despair with particularly high unemployment locally. These grim municipal tenements known locally as the Four Squares did nothing to improve the environment and were demolished in 1977.

The Great Eastern pub on Langsdale Street survived the clearance of the rest of the area.
Regrettably it closed in 1983 making the future of this impressive building uncertain.

Kempston Street was once the area from where Liverpool entertainer Frankie Vaughan hailed. These 'landing' houses dating from 1902 had side flights of stairs and landings at the rear. This area is now designated for commercial and industrial use.

This warehouselike block was in fact housing and stood on Greenside until 1965. There can be no argument over the decision to pull down this appalling housing.

Nearby Back College Street also provided very poor conditions and deserved to be condemned. The back of this terrace was just a long blank wall containing no windows at all.

There are very few of these raised terraces left today though in the 1960s they were still quite common. Talbot Street shown here was demolished in the late 1960s. Yates Street and Corn Street in the Dingle provide surviving examples.

The Blue Ball pub was named with reference to the police station next door to it on Prescot Street. The Royal Liverpool Hospital now occupies virtually all one side of the street facing and the pub was demolished in 1977 to make way for the hospital. Many Merseybeat groups performed at the Blue Ball in the 1950s/60s

Gloucester Place off Low Hill contained this later 'landing' block with the landing at the higher level and dormer windows to light the attics. Unlike the others shown here the landing is not over shops but more houses, thus built one on top of the other.

This landing block stood behind the Hippodrome Cinema on Winter Street. Here, the stairs to this shorter block are at one end.

The houses on the left hand side of Rockwood Street which stood near Farnworth Street were obviously the 'posh' ones with bay windows, cellars and an attic floor in some.

This lamp standard in Fedora Street off West Derby Road has not been treated with much respect. This terrace had the uncommon feature of a tiled canopy over the ground floor windows.

This landing block on Boaler Street was demolished in 1967. It was obviously in a poor state but it seems sad that its unusual features of central flights of stairs and landing canopies have been lost.

The Sacred Heart Church on Hall Lane can be seen in the background of this photograph of Ambrose Street. The houses have long gone and a new road scheme may mean the end for the church too.

Tillotson Street off Hall Street had 3 storey terraces which unusually had no cellars.

The Royal Liverpool Hospital occupies the site of Bengal Street. It is interesting to note, in the rear shot, that the terraces in the foreground have no back windows whilst the rest of the street did. The corner of the Vernon Arms pub is just visible (see below).

In the early nineteenth century 'Vernon's Hall' stood here and from this Mount Vernon was named. The Lybro Factory was a well-known landmark until its demolition in 1983. The tower to the right is that of St Mary's Church, one of the earliest city churches built in 1812.

Albert Terrace, off Queensland Street, was a block with three storeys at the front sloping to two at the back. This terrace was demolished in the 1960s and new housing built in the area; this too is now being demolished.

This row of shops had very small flats rather than houses over it. It stood at the top of Smithdown Lane until 1968.

Bamber Street nearby had poor housing which deserved demolition. These streets were dominated by the large chimney which was a ventilation shaft for the early railway system.

Islington L3 - *The whole north side of Islington was demolished in the 1970s for road widening. This was one of the blocks of early town houses in the course of demolition when photographed in 1970, two workmen can be seen on the roof as the demolition was in progress. (aerial view on page 107).*

Moss Street L6 - *A 1960s view of the west side of Moss Street, which runs from Islington to London Road, two pubs are shown between shops, the nearest was the Cottage, which was listed 104 Devon Street, on whose corner the pub stood, and the other was the Prince Hotel, listed 13b Moss Street and 117 Kempston Street, both now long demolished.*

Moss Street L6 - *Partially shown on the previous photograph, this block as far as London Road, was a long established business as indicated, and was awaiting demolition when photographed in 2003, apartments having since been constructed on this site. The taller building shown at the junction with London Road was a former pub, the Prince of Wales. Although no longer a pub, its façade has been retained amongst new property.*

London Road L3 - *Featuring the last block on the north side of the Road in 2002, just short of the previously named Prince of Wales, all empty shops awaiting demolition, with the last building at the corner of Falkland Street a former pub, the Kings Arms, all since demolished, and replaced by accommodation.*

Warburton Street L7 - *Located off Mount Vernon Street, large three storey dwellings photographed in 1968 shortly before demolition. The site of the former street is now part of a car park for the Royal Liverpool University Hospital.*

Crown Street L7 - *Large two storey Victorian houses in this view from 1967, during demolition. This long thoroughfare originally ran from Pembroke Place in the City Centre, to Upper Parliament Street, a distance of 1,422 yards, since physically broken up, and buildings connected to the University now in abundance in the vicinity (a separate view is on page 168).*

Mulberry Street L7 - *The old houses still standing and a former PH, the Myrtle, numbered 105/107 Mulberry Street, at the junction of Myrtle Street when photographed in 1965. Another pub, the Myrtle Hotel was nearby, numbered 71 Myrtle Street, all now just a memory, and as with the latter, university buildings are abundant in the vicinity (The Myrtle Hotel is featured derelict on page 168).*

Myrtle Street L7 - *Also from the 1960s, showing a derelict building next door to a pub, the Portland Arms, junction of Melville Place, and still trading then, before eventual demolition. On the other side of Melville Place is a portion of Myrtle Gardens (see next view).*

Myrtle Gardens L7 - *Showing the inter-war block of tenements during demolition in the early 1980s, on Myrtle Street, although a portion of the flats fronting Melville Place, were retained, and refurbished as Minster Court.*

Chatsworth Street L7 - *Formerly running between Wavertree Road and Smithdown Lane, containing a mixture of 3 and 2 storey houses, having front gardens on this section when photographed during demolition in 1968, the thoroughfare since broken up, with a section now named Chatsworth Drive.*

Sophia Street L7
Photographed in 1968, when this street, and many of the surrounding streets were being demolished, located between Smithdown Lane and Chatsworth Street, and was 145 yards in length. There are more modern houses now in this area.

Squires Street L7
A snow covered area fronting the street when photographed in 1969, formerly located between Chatsworth Street and Queensland Street, now long demolished.

Palmerston Street L7
Another of the many terraced streets around the Chatsworth Street area. Although housing was built to replace the numerous old terraced streets here from the late 1960s and 70s, the actual site of this street, and the next, remained as a "buffet" of open grassland until after the new millennium, when new housing was built on the site, adjacent to the west side of Tunnel Road.

Clarendon Street L7
This street ran from Chatsworth Street to Tunnel Road, partly shown at the end, and was 85 yards long; photographed during demolition in 1967.

Woodside Street L7 - *Located off Wavertree Road when photographed in 1968, as demolition is ongoing. The frontage of the main road can be seen in the distance, and parts of the frontage of Wavertree Road itself have recently been demolished.*

Lennox Street L7 - *One of a cluster of former terraced streets close to Kensington and Holt Road, formerly located between Solomon Street and Cotswold Street in the 1960s; modern houses and open grassland now in this region (see next view).*

Gilead Street L7 (2 views)

The Liver Vaults Pub over four decades - listed 59/63 Gilead Street, off Kensington, and on the gable end of this 1960s view a sign reads "Balm Street Passage" a former alley, 83 yards long, that ran from Balm Street alongside the pub to Lennox Street, and had recently been demolished in this view, the sign on the frontage of the pub was Ind Coope (Brewer). This Brewery merged with Joshua Tetley in 1960 to form Tetley Walker Ltd, and was later part of the Allied Breweries Group. See also an advert on the wall for a former drink, "Double Diamond".

2011

The houses southward still remain, whereas northward were demolished, and the sign for new property is Lennox Way, with Gilead Street re-aligned. The section of the old alley alongside the pub now fenced off, with a new wall in place, and the old alley sign long gone, and the gable end now showing a Tetley sign, with the pub's name displayed.

Plimsoll Street L7 - *Although only photographed in 2006, this property, off Durning Road, has since been demolished, as with all the surrounding property, a former local PH, the Grove, is featured at the top, on Hawthorn Grove.*

Royston Arms PH - *Standing derelict when photographed in 2007, located close to the above picture, since demolished. It was numbered 66 Royston Street, and 54 Dorothy Street, and both streets have recently been demolished.*

The Upper Parliament Street Area
(1986)

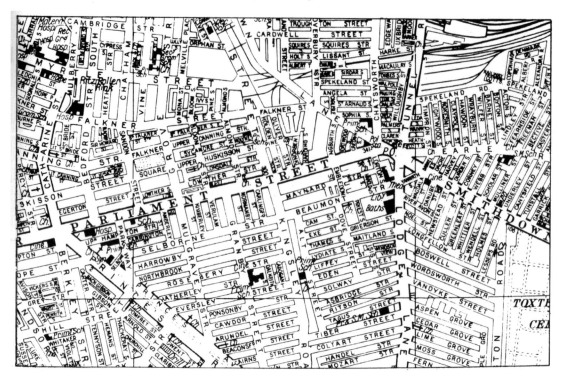

The Toxteth district grew at the end of the 18th and beginning of the 19th centuries as one of the fashionable parts of Liverpool in which wealthy merchants established themselves amongst parks at the edge of the old city. For centuries old Liverpool was bounded by Toxteth Park and the villages of West Derby, Everton and Kirkdale. Toxteth Park was actually a royal forest which was 'disparked' in 1591 and the township of Toxteth was established in 1640. Its absorption into the suburbs of Liverpool came with the growth of Liverpool's prosperity and the housing aspirations of the city's wealthy during the 1800s. Toxteth today still has many fine Georgian and early Victorian houses, although a vast number of original ones were allowed to decay and have vanished. As recently as the 1970s entire streets and terraces were demolished, notably in the area around the University as the campus expanded into the Grove Street and Myrtle Street region. Other principal roads, squares and boulevards suffered major losses and only in the last few years have attempts been made to restore and renovate what remains. Upper Parliament Street might be seen as an example of this 'eleventh hour' shift of policy.

Upper Parliament Street was laid out on the old boundary between Liverpool and Toxteth and runs eastwards from the river and the old 18th century city. This route begins near the river as Parliament Street, named in 1773, as part of what was then the new township of Harrington. Parliament Street had been known, appropriately enough as 'Townsend Lane' prior to this date. The name 'Harrington' gradually disappeared as Liverpool expanded and the Toxteth district rapidly developed during the late 18th and early 19th century. In the eastern parts of this growing district elegant squares and substantial terraces were established. On present day Grove Street stands a recently renovated block of Georgian dwellings which makes up a section of Falkner Square, one of the few remaining squares in Liverpool. On either side of this block now stands new housing, where until the 1960s stood Georgian houses similar to those still in evidence on the opposite side of Grove Street. Most of Abercrombie Square off Oxford Street – a particularly splendid example – has survived as part of the University accommodation. Behind the elegant squares, along narrower streets and alleys off the broader roads and boulevards, numerous more humble dwellings were built. Examples of this aspect of Toxteth can be seen in the photographs – Mona Street and Bloom Street behind the more fashionable and prominent Myrtle Street and on narrow Florist Street lying behind the grander Grove Street and Crown Street. Many other earlier and often smaller terraced houses had long been regarded as slums, yet handsome good quality housing – much of it late Georgian – has been unnecessarily cleared along with the sub-standard and derelict.

An obvious example of the poorer cramped housing from the 1960s was Aigburth Street (see page 170) in the area at the very top of Upper Parliament Street. The original infamous slums of this area, especially further towards Smithdown Lane, dated from the 1830s and much of this was not cleared until the 1930s. This district was particularly badly overcrowded and squalid during the 1830s. Barton Lane, which ran where Entwistle Heights now stands, had 5 unnamed courts though it was only 80 yards long. This was probably the largest area of slum housing outside the city boundary at that time. Yet the 'slum clearance' programmes of the sixties produced very dubious results, as 'high rise' blocks took over from the terraced streets. Entwistle Heights (in photo with Milner House) was the highest of the multi-storey flats when it was opened in 1964. Twenty years later this and many similar flats are due for demolition. Others have already been taken down.

Opinions will probably always differ as to precisely which houses and streets were best demolished and which should have been preserved. But surely the type represented by Longsdale Street (see page 170) for example has never been replaced by anything remotely comparable in quality or appeal? Leaving aside the question of the much despised tower block, even the new houses that stand on the cleared sites of many of Toxteth's former streets would not bear comparison to the original ones had they been renovated. The wisdom of so much of the redevelopment in the fifties and sixties is certainly questionable when we see – as the photo of Upper Hill Street shows (see page 197) – as new, some twenty years on, being demolished alongside the old.

Cumberland Terrace, Upper Parliament Street was built in 1847 and was demolished in 1978 whilst neighbouring blocks were being renovated.

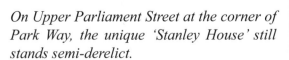
On Upper Parliament Street at the corner of Park Way, the unique 'Stanley House' still stands semi-derelict.

Upper Parliament Street, a listed building and a splendid example of the Georgian houses that were typical of the area. It was demolished in the 1980s to make way for the inner ring road.

A mid-Victorian terrace which stood in Crown Street until the 1960s. This section of the street has now been completely cleared and landscaped.

Myrtle Street from the corner of Vine Street. The municipal flats standing beyond the junction with Grove Street have survived whilst similar ones have been demolished. These flats have been renovated and sold by a private developer. The corner block in the forefront is the Myrtle Street Hotel PH, 146 Vine Street, awaiting demolition.

Bloom Street, off Myrtle Street, showing modest but well-built terraces with cellars and small front gardens.

Mona Street off Myrtle Street in an advanced state of decay in the 1960s.

This once-elegant terrace of three-storey houses with basements stood in Vine Street until the late 1960s. The entire street has since been cleared and is now part of the University campus.

Large Georgian houses in Grove Street at the junction with Falkner Street.

Three-storey terraced houses, cramped dwellings with no rear windows, standing on old Florist Street which ran between Grove Street and Crown Street. Cleared in 1967, only the Oxford pub remains.

Lonsdale Street, shown here in 1969. These modest terraces had many fine features and very few examples of these well-built houses survive today. St Nathaniel's Church, seen in the background, dates from the 1860s and still stands today amidst new housing.

Elegant Georgian houses in Upper Huskisson Street, like too many others they never survived the 1960s.

Aigburth Street, typical of the poorer housing at the top of elegant Upper Parliament Street. Photographed in 1967, Milner House flats are being constructed on the cleared site, with Entwistle Heights which opened in 1965 towering in the background. Both blocks are now due for demolition.

Exe Street, typical of the nineteenth century two-up two-down terraced houses cleared from many parts of the city in the 1960s. Many similar properties survive still, particularly in the Lodge Lane area.

Beaumont Street, off Lodge Lane, in an area of Toxteth which was once known as 'Windsor'. These mid-Victorian houses were demolished in 1969 to make way for new housing.

Many Victorian houses built in the 1870s survive in various states of repair in Princes Road. The prestigious residential boulevard was originally laid out in 1846 to run from Upper Parliament Street southwards to Princes Park. It is interesting to note that this dual carriageway has two names: the southbound road is Princes Avenue while the northbound is Princes Road.

Vronhill Street, off High Park Street was cleared in the early 1980s.

A scene which sums up much about the modern inner city, evoking for many people a mixture of sadness, nostalgia and anger. The last survivor of the original buildings on Upper Hill Street, another old local – The Grecian Pub – stands closed whilst the sub-standard flats and houses which surround it are being demolished after only twenty year's service. Another clearer view on page 197.

Stanhope Cottages (1902) in Upper Stanhope Street were demolished in the late 1960s.

The David Lewis Building was another fine building demolished during the building of the inner ring road. It stood at St Georges Place between St James Place and Great George Street.

These larger Georgian houses on St James Road, shown here from the rear, were demolished in the late 1960s along with the poorer, cramped two-storey terraces lower down the slope on the river side of the Anglican Cathedral.

Sands Street South, on the slope running down to Great George Street, lies in the shadow of the Anglican Cathedral towering above.

Dingle
(1986)

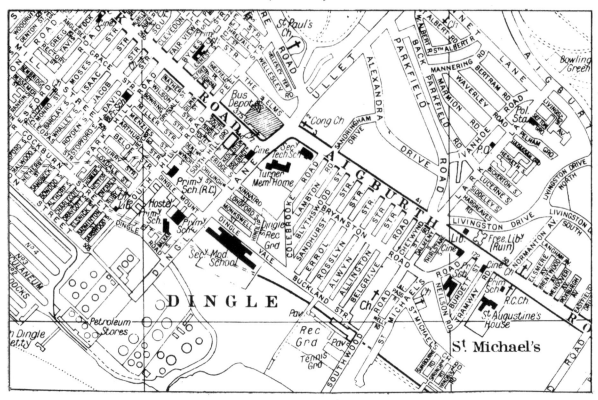

The Dingle area of Liverpool is south of the city centre, close to the once thriving south docks complex. This location has meant that over the years the Dingle has provided living accommodation for many people working in dock related industries.

Examples of several types of early municipal housing can be found here. Many were occupied until the 1960s but most have fortunately now been demolished. Ironically it is some of the earliest housing here, such as the terrace shown in Dingle Lane, which seems most likely to survive. This terrace would have been luxurious compared with the 'courts' that pre-existed it. The same can be said of virtually all the examples shown here even though they were of a poor standard by 1960's expectations. Recently the emphasis has been on landscaping derelict land and building low density housing. The riverside International Garden Festival 1984 site borders onto Dingle and provides a splendid example of creative reclamation of a totally derelict and polluted stretch of land.

Dingle Lane runs from the end of Park Road towards the Mersey and provides an excellent example of worthwhile renovation. The terrace is early for the area as the plaque set into the sandstone wall indicates, it reads: Borough of Liverpool, erected by the Health Committee 1865.

These 2 tenement blocks at the Aigburth end of Park Road date from 1923 when they were considered to be fine housing. Both Dingle House and South Hill House are currently scheduled for demolition.

This view of the Dingle tenements shows clearly their proximity to the International Garden Festival site.

Close by the tenements is Dingle Mount, a block of walk-up flats built in the 1930s but nearing the end of its life.

South Street ran from Princes Gate at the entrance to Princes Park to Park Road in the Dingle. This section of handsome mid-Victorian houses with gardens at the Park Road end of South Street disappeared in 1966.

These substantial 3 storey terraces in Harlow Street were demolished in the 1960s although it has taken until the mid-1980s for replacement housing to be built.

A general view of the Pecksniff and Micawber Street area; streets near Park Road were named after Dickens' characters. This poor housing, long overdue for demolition, finally went in the early 1980s.

This 'landing' house was built in 1913 and lasted until the late 1960s. It stood in Northumberland Street which runs between Windsor Street and Sefton Street.

Warwick Gardens tenement block was one of the many municipal blocks of flats in the Dingle area. It stood at the junction of Caryl Street and Warwick Street.

A lone Georgian house standing in Stanhope Street shortly before demolition.

Beaufort Street, off Stanhope Street, grim, far from elegant terraced houses.

South of the City Centre

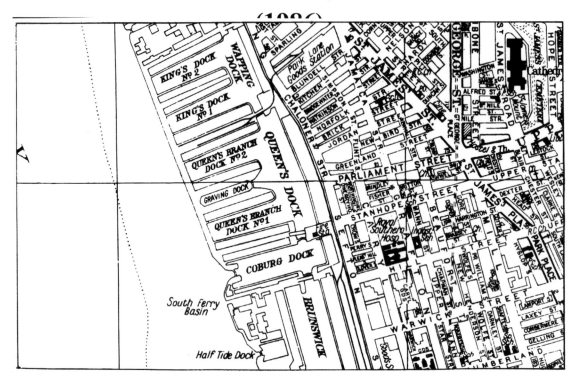

The proximity of this area to the city centre and Liverpool's earliest docks made it, in the past, one of the city's most busy and prosperous areas. Regrettably, this is difficult to imagine from its appearance today. Even more regrettable is that so much of the area's decline and demolition has occurred within the last 25 years.

Liverpool's original harbour known as the Pool was fed by a creek which ran along the line of Whitechapel and Paradise Street. Although plans for a dock had been considered as early as 1561 it was not until 1715 that the conversion of the Pool into the Old Dock was completed. This dock was filled in in 1826 and its site is now occupied by the Canning Place block. Canning Dock was built in 1737 as a basin for the Old Dock and the Salthouse Dock following in 1753. In fact neither dock was initially known by these names; Canning Dock was not named until its reconstruction in 1813 and Salthouse Dock was first called South Dock and renamed later in the century after the saltworks which stood nearby. There is also a street named after the salt works. The stretch of docks from Herculaneum, now filled, to the Pier Head has seen virtually no commercial traffic since the early 1970s. Gone are the ships carrying cargoes of fruit into the King's Docks which I myself remember unloading in 1969. As the docks fell into disrepair many fine buildings on the dock estate and the dock road went with them. For instance, the fine Dukes Dock warehouse, which was built by French prisoners of war in 1811, some 35 years earlier than the neighbouring Albert Dock warehouses, was demolished in 1966. But at last attitudes seem to be changing. The injection of central government funds via the Merseyside Development Corporation has provided money to buy the South Docks estate from the Mersey Docks and Harbour Company. The estate is now being reclaimed from dereliction and developed as a new industrial and recreation area. The flagship of this scheme is the Albert Dock where a massive restoration scheme is underway. It is a wonderful venture which not only preserves a major building but part of our maritime history at the same time. Both the

Albert and the fine Wapping Warehouse have been threatened with demolition but their future is now secure.

The tragedy is that so many buildings have already been lost. On the other side of the dock road virtually nothing is left of Liverpool's maritime history apart from street names and a handful of pubs and warehouses. All of what was once the heart of 'Sailor Town' around Canning Place has vanished. From the days of sail this district had a notorious reputation the world over but now no vestige of it remains. Many of these losses almost amount to vandalism on the part of the 'City Fathers'. It is only in the last decade that the authorities have woken up and are now striving to protect some of the remaining monuments to Liverpool's past. At least one corner of Liverpool, the Albert Dock, has some hope for the future.

The dock road south of the city centre has several names: Strand Street, Wapping, Chaloner Street and finally Sefton Street. There was reputed to be a pub on almost every corner of which we show four. The first is the Queens Dock Hotel which ended its life as a canteen before demolition.

The Brunswick known locally as the 'Seven Steps', is also named after an adjacent dock. This pub is still standing, though empty and derelict.

The Baltic Fleet pub is an imposing listed building and the quality of its architecture has probably saved it. Renovations have been carried out since this photograph was taken in 1976.

The Duke's Crown pub, though another fine building, failed to survive the new ring road scheme.

In Park Lane stood what was latterly known as the Keans Hotel. This magnificent example of a highly decorated Victorian building is sadly no longer standing. As the lettering shows it was originally built for a wine and spirits business who probably required premises close to the bonded warehouses at Albert Dock.

This shot of the Baltic Ship's Stores shows another building on Park Lane whose use was dock related.

Behind this part of Park Lane is an area of municipal tenements. Kent Gardens from the 1930s is shown here and even this building has a maritime history. The flats occupy the former site of the Phoenix foundry where Merseyside's first marine engine was built. Lydia Anne Street was named after the foundry manager's wife.

These tenements in the same area date from the 1920s and were amongst the first dwellings to replace the overcrowded, squalid courts that were rife in the district.

Brick Street ran east-west between St James Street and Chaloner Street. Originally it was dense with the old Liverpool courts, later a mixture of industrial units and older municipal flats existed, such as Prince Albert Gardens in St James Street pictured here during demolition in 1981.

This once magnificent building on Hurst Street has also been lost. Pictured here at the end of its life, this highly ornate piece of Victoriana would surely have been worth saving as its like will never be built again.

The cross roads of Hurst Street and Salthouse Lane shows some of the original housing dating from the mid-nineteenth century. These narrow houses had one room per floor built over cellars; they were not graced with rear windows.

South Castle Street was almost totally destroyed by bombing during the last war. This last surviving block was destroyed by the planners and came down in 1974 and now the street itself no longer exists.

King Street has also disappeared and these imposing warehouses made way for the 'Holiday Inn' Hotel.

Opposite King Street stood Chapel Walk and Benn's Gardens; these narrow streets also tragically disappeared in the early 1970s with no thought of preserving these interesting buildings.

The area had much charm and the fine terraces were used as small business premises. The two streets formed a four sided block opening off South Castle Street and were even enclosed with their own wrought iron gates.

The Sailors Home dating from 1847, was one of Liverpool's most magnificent and well known buildings. The design of the interior was also interesting with decks reminiscent of sailing ships. It was demolished in 1973.

The Flying Dutchman, named after a seafarers legend, stood close to the site of Liverpool's first dock at the corner of Canning Place and Litherland Alley.

This warehouse stood on Crooked Lane until 1975. This winding alley was part of the network of lanes that existed in the Canning Place area. The Albert Dock is clearly visible in the background.

(1975)

These photographs show one of the few buildings that looks better in 1985 than it did in 1975. The Albert Dock warehouse complex is the largest single area of Grade 1 listed buildings in the country. Thanks to the intervention of the Merseyside Development Corporation the Albert Dock is being completely renovated and re-developed.

It is once more buzzing with activity it houses shops, offices, flats, restaurants and bars as well as the Tate Gallery Liverpool and the Maritime Museum.

(1985)

(2013)

The successful renovatic here demonstrate the so worth of utilising these buildings for both highlighting Liverpool's heritage and paving the way for its future.

South Liverpool 1 and 8

Incorporating the previous sections Upper Parliament Street, South of City Centre and Dingle from original Tumbling Down book.

The vicinity both east and west of Park Lane and St James Street was a most squalid part of Liverpool in the 19th century. The western side was mainly cleared of the slums as the century progressed with the majority being replaced by warehouses and industrial units (see Brick Street page 184). In common with other inner-city areas, some of the squalid conditions remained well into the 20th century.

Shaw's Alley/Sparling Street L1 *- This view c.1904, at the northern end of Shaw's Alley. On the left three storey cellar dwellings in the course of being cleared for demolition. Although it's possible they were still housing families looking at the number of children in this photograph, they were finally replaced by 1930s built houses.*

Maghull Street *- This view is the southern end of Shaw's Alley, from Maghull Street, of which only the name plate remains when photographed in 1999. Previously 50 yards in length from Hurst Street to Shaw's Alley, the warehouses shown on the right have been demolished, whereas the warehouses on Shaw's Alley remain to date, having replaced the slums many years ago.*

Liverpool's Chinatown, the oldest in Europe, is now mainly confined to the Nelson Street vicinity, defined by a magnificient Chinese arch erected in 2000.

During the 19th century and first half of the 20th century it extended a lot further, and the following five photographs were taken in the midst of Chinatown.

Pitt Street/Dickenson Street L1
A former PH, the Star surrounded by 3 storey dwellings when photographed c.1912. Note the court entrance adjoining the pub, a common occurrence in those days. (See Grapes PH, Roscoe Street/ Knight Street, City Centre page 227). Most of this vicinity was demolished during the 1920s, although several survived until the 1960s.

St James Street L1 - *Featuring a pub, the Royal, number 38 and 1 Bridgewater Street, when photographed in 1985, one of formerly 14 on the thoroughfare. It's currently closed, last in use as a newsagent's. The warehouses shown remain to date.*

Horse Shoe PH L1 - *Number 24 Duncan Street off St James Street, and photographed c.1908, when the original houses were still standing either side of the pub.*

Horse Shoe PH L1 - *The same pub in 2006, empty and boarded up by this date, and still retaining its horseshoe shaped door. The more modern structure to the right of the pub, a former housing office has also been demolished, and since replaced with flats, and the pub has also since been demolished.*

Duncan Street/Upper Frederick Street L1

A block of comparatively modern houses awaiting demolition when photographed in 2002. Almost facing the previous view, a former pub, The Letters, is shown on the right, still standing at 109/111 St James Street.

View L1 & L8

Photographed in 1977, this view is from St James Place, Liverpool 8 into Liverpool 1, and with the exception of the Beacon in the distance, and the building on the extreme left, all have been demolished. The building on the left has listed status, number 3/4 Great George Place, originally built for the North and South Wales Bank, later the Midland Bank, and this fine Victorian structure has had various uses since closing as a Bank. The adjoining former PH, the Lord Nelson, *has been demolished, likewise the comparatively modern houses on Great George Street.*

The block on the right was number 1 Upper Parliament Street, a fine example of a Georgian house that was listed. However, it was demolished for one of the many proposed schemes that never materialised, a new ring road to the City Centre, whereas the building in the centre, the David Lewis Building, although not listed, is another example of a fine structure succumbing to the bulldozer, see page 168 top left.

Upper Parliament Street L8

Another fine Georgian block, a little higher up than the previous view, sadly, in a dilapidated state and seemingly waiting for the bulldozer when photographed in 1999. However, this fate was avoided, and the block has since been renovated, and remains to date.

Stanhope St./ Caryl St. L8

This is the Angel PH, numbered 27-29 at the junction with Caryl Street and still open when photographed in 1998. Partly shown is Cains Brewery, still operating (described in more detail in volume 1, Pub in Every corner). This pub has been closed for some years now yet still stands derelict in 2012.

Chesterfield Street L8

A 1930s built block of tenements named Stanhope House, located between Upper Parliament Street and Upper Stanhope Street. The Anglican Cathedral pictured behind when photographed in 1989, as the tenements lay empty, awaiting demolition.

Berkley Street L8

Located between Upper Parliament Street and Upper Stanhope Street, this block of dilapidated dwellings were actually listed Georgian Houses The higher structure in the forefront was listed as 123 Upper Stanhope Street, with the remainder 2 -12 Berkley Street. At the other end of the block is another higher structure which was in Hampton Street (see next view) but sadly, like so many other listed buildings, this status did not save them. Photographed in 1999, and demolished soon after, open grassland currently occupies this site.

Hampton Street L8

Partially seen in the previous photograph, this street runs from Windsor Street to Berkley Street, with the dilapidated huge block number 68 Hampton Street, also photographed in 1999, and demolished at the same time as the previous view. Shown in Berkley Street is the listed Greek Orthodox Church 1865-1870, a fine example of a Byzantine style building, boasting their distinctive domes, with one of them fully and one partly shown in this view.

Catharine Street/Canning Street L8

Featuring a former Presbyterian Church in the course of demolition when photographed in 1987. The Georgian Houses on the right remain.

Falkner Street L8

This long thoroughfare led eastward from the edge of Liverpool 8 at Hope Street in the City Centre, to the top of Smithdown Lane at Edge Hill, Liverpool 7. Georgian properties remain at the City Centre end. This block was demolished in the 1960s, before such property was appreciated.

Falkner Street L8

The street has been physically broken up since the time of the previous view, with the Women's Hospital having been constructed over part of it. Nearer the eastern end stood more humble housing, and this PH, the Crown, with haphazard "under new management" signs displayed was numbered 226 Falkner Street, at the junction of Holden Street when photographed in 1991, and now long demolished.

Oliver Street L8

This was one of a cluster of terraced streets in the vicinity, next to Holden Street between Falkner Street and Upper Parliament Street when photographed in 1967, all now long gone.

Two era's of Upper Hill Street

Phoenix Inn L8
This view from the 1920s shows the pub, formerly number 23, at the junction with Wesley Street. On the left is a shop advertising Hovis, which was at the junction of Clarke Street, note the "young" tree near the gas light. This area was mainly cleared in the 1960s.

Grecian PH L8
In 1988 higher up the street, the pub now derelict. The high rise flats on the left, and maisonettes on the right that replaced the houses from the previous view are now being demolished. Modern houses now proliferate the area, with the street having been physically split up from when it originally ran from St James Place to Princes Road when it was 668 yards long.

Pecksniff Street L8
This street was between North Hill Street and Northumberland Street, when photographed in 1978, one of a cluster of streets in the vicinity that were demolished in the 1980s and modern houses now stand in this area. Many of them, including this one, were named after Dickens' characters.

The following three photographs are located off the south side of High Park Street (Welsh Streets). The old houses off the north side (Welsh Streets) were demolished in the 1980s (see Vronhill Street page 171).

Voelas Street L8 - *Sections of the street already demolished when photographed in 2012, so presumably demolition of the rest seem likely.*

Kinmel Street L8
This view looking towards High Park Street is from 2012, and all but empty, so similar to the last view in that demolition seems likely.

Madryn Street L8

Another street in this vicinity, all but empty awaiting demolition, similar to the nearby Granby Street area, and City wide such as the Anfield and Bootle areas, all having suffered years of uncertainty, that should have been resolved years ago, but haven't and still ongoing in most cases. Perhaps this particular street or at least one house anyway, should be preserved. And that's because it's the birthplace of Ringo Starr (Richard Starky). Like him or loathe him, it is still the birthplace of a "Beatle" and the gravy train that is the Beatles' legacy, still goes on making money through tourism for the City. Before going to print I believe the house is to be saved, although how many others is still uncertain. Presumably demolition will still go ahead for some, and as it's still not actually verified, the fate of these houses is beyond the scope of this book.

Melville Street L8
This street still remains off High Park Street, beyond the Welsh Streets nearer to Park Road, although the houses featured are now long gone. They were a mixture of two and three storey houses when photographed in 1969.

Second View: The two storey houses of Melville Street having been demolished when photographed later in 1969. Across the entry are the rear of the houses of the former Twiss Street, since demolished, and the tower in the background is part of the High Park Street Reservoir, built in 1855, and which still stands today. Familiar to generations of scousers and clearly shown in the forefront is a former "back yard toilet". Still in common use up until the late 1960s (and possibly beyond).

Almost facing High Park Street across Princes Road/Princes Avenue is the Granby Street area, where the following are situated.

Cairns Street L8 - *Photographed in 2006, when empty and boarded up, and seemingly due for demolition, but like so many other inner City areas, streets are left derelict sometimes for years, leaving residents in limbo as to the fate of their homes.*

Second view L8: This is the same street in 2012, six years later, still empty and boarded up, but there is a difference to the previous view, the houses have all been painted, making it look tidier, and flower beds have been put in place, so what does that mean, demolition or renovation? This book will probably be in print before anything happens, although by "sprucing" the street up, renovation seems a possibility, doesn't it!

Jermyn Street L8 - This street in the same situation as the previous one, photographed in 2012, and at the time of writing still uncertain as to its fate, although the two houses minus their frontage will probably have to be demolished.

Beaconsfield Street L8 - *Similar to Cairns Street, these empty houses having been painted, so keeping it "tidy" and like the surrounding streets their fate may well be beyond the scope of this publication.*

Granby Street L8: As I've mentioned elsewhere in this publication, (see Stanley Road, Kirkdale) numerous three storey blocks of shops were the centre of communities from the surrounding streets for generations throughout the inner City areas. Particularly since the 1960s they have been demolished on a massive scale as the old communities were broken up, and into the second decade of the 21st Century, it's the turn of this part of Liverpool 8.

The previous streets cut across Granby Street, once a bustling thriving community, now sadly nearly all gone, with the following two, three-storey blocks still standing awaiting their fate when photographed in 2011. Currently new houses have been constructed, with open grassland, and the streets shown awaiting their fate.

Granby Street L8
All boarded up awaiting the inevitable, this block is between Arundel Street and Cawdor Street when photographed in 2011.

Granby Street L8
This block, the next one along, is between Cawdor Street and Ponsonby Street; note the new houses further along, where another former three storey block used to stand.

Lodge Lane L8 - *This view from 2006 features a former PH the Sportsman in a derelict state, despite being a modern structure, and has since been demolished. It had replaced an earlier pub, The Coach and Horses. The site has now been landscaped.*

The previous photographs south of the top end of the Upper Parliament area, and west of the Lodge Lane area, was long known as the "Windsor" district of Liverpool 8, the following are closer to the river in Liverpool 8, the Dingle area.

Park Road L8 - *A long major road through Dingle, and as just described in Granby Street, and others such as Stanley Road in Kirkdale, as the old streets vanished, and the people moved out, so too did the three storey blocks of the main road that catered for the needs of the local population. This was one such block, located between Peel Street and Leonora Street when photographed in 1986, and since demolished, like the majority of the frontage of the road; some still remain, and the adjoining block on this view is one such block, the corner building was a former PH, the Dingle (featured in* A Pub On Every Corner Volume 2) *currently a Funeral Parlour.*

Hawkstone Street L8
Originally running from Peel Street to South Street, east of Park Road when the old property existed, then physically split in the 1960s when these houses were built, and a portion of South Street was demolished. Another example of comparatively modern houses awaiting demolition when photographed in 1999, so common throughout the inner City areas.

Greig Street L8
One of numerous terraced streets off the west side of Park Road in the 1960s, formerly leading down to Rectory Street, and in the course of being demolished when photographed in 1967, both named streets now long demolished.

Royal Oak PH L8
Standing at the junction of Park Place and Upper Warwick Street, this view is from the 1920s, and the pub was destroyed and replaced with a pub of the same name in the 1950s. Although recently opened, it's currently closed, a trend so common of late throughout the City, and beyond. The pub is one of only a few along this stretch of the thoroughfare from the start of Liverpool 8; St James Place, Park Place, and Park Road, which together contained over 30 pubs in the 1960s and earlier.

Mill Street L8
Similar to Park Road in that most of the old three storey blocks have been demolished, this derelict block was at the corner of Warwick Street, and last in use as a betting shop as shown, photographed in 1989. The site is now landscaped amongst modern houses.

Great Eastern PH L8 - Number 342 Mill Street, this view is from the 1950s, featured in Volume 2 of my Pub Books. I will repeat what I recorded about this Pub's name in the book: *'named after the great eastern steamship, the biggest ship in the world when launched in 1858, although the ship was of a revolutionary design, having many new features, she was a failure, largely through financial mismanagement. Three other Liverpool pubs also had the same name, to be found in Cockspur Street, 13, Langsdale Street, 13, and Scotland Road, 15. A former mast of the ship became a flagpole at the Kop end of Liverpool Football Club's ground.*

King Gardens L8 - *Tenements on Mill Street photographed in 1986 when empty and awaiting demolition, as described. Elsewhere in this publication, due to the chronic housing shortage after the war, tenements such as these were constructed in the style of the earlier built 1930s tenements, and were completed in 1949.*

Brunswick Gardens L8 - *1930s built tenements formerly on Caryl Street, between Northumberland Street and Park Street such property was prevalent in this part of south Liverpool; close by stood Warwick Gardens and Caryl Gardens.*

Singleton Arms PH L8 - *Still displaying its name when photographed in 1992, although empty and boarded up. It was named after the Liverpool boxer, Joey Singleton, and was earlier named the Little Woodman.*

Hill Street/Sefton Street L8 - *The building almost demolished was the former Highland Home Hotel, listed at 6/8 Hill Street, a long established dock side pub about to bite the dust when photographed in 1998. The structure on the other side of Hill Street is the previously named pub, still derelict, with the name having been removed by this time surprisingly, into 2012, and the structure still remains, although currently still derelict.*

Wilson King Mill L3 - *This former huge silo was in the Brunswick Dock, and a well-known land mark pre-1990s. The huge concrete built silo was constructed in 1936, and photographed here shortly before demolition in 1989. An earlier built silo is shown further along during demolition, having been constructed in 1906.*

Riverside Drive L17 - *This view from 1984 was part of the International Garden Festival site. Although a popular attraction at the time, it was allowed to fall into disuse, and amazingly remained derelict for over 25 years! Then after numerous false dawns, it was finally re-opened in 2012, although not on the scale of the original.*

Festival Bus L1
Passengers in Lime Street, City Centre, boarding the "Festival Bus" in 1984.

City Centre
(1986)

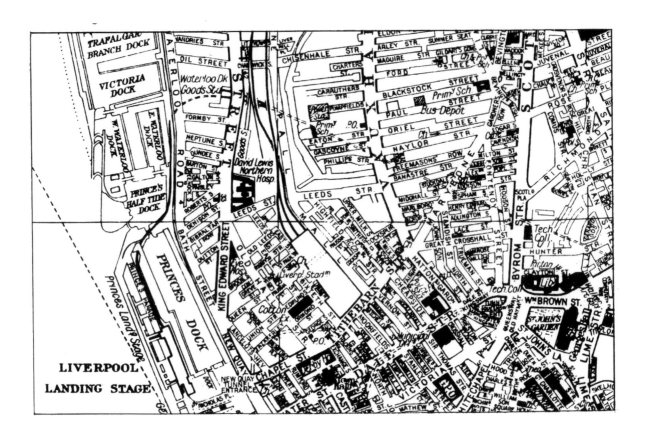

Much of the old city centre has disappeared in the last twenty years as the photographs in this book remind us. Not only have we lost many fine buildings but thriving, bustling communities centred around markets have vanished too. The extent of the changes has often been drastic, as in Marybone; sometimes piecemeal, as in Tithebarn Street. For example, the buildings opposite Exchange Station have recently been cleared but fortunately the station's original façade has been restored and preserved as part of a new building complex which now stands on the site of the old station. Tithebarn Street is one of old Liverpool's original streets. Formerly known as Moor Street it was re-named after the erection of a tythe barn in 1523, probably on the site of Marybone's junction with Great Crosshall Street. Marybone was once a densely populated corner of the city, one of the poorest areas of nineteenth century Liverpool. Many of its streets have now disappeared under the new inner ring road.

Other areas have undergone changes perhaps less worthwhile. In Great Charlotte Street which formerly ran from Whitechapel to Ranelagh Street there used to be three markets. Whilst several adjacent streets simply disappeared, Great Charlotte Street was reduced to a small section standing between Ranelagh Street and Elliott Street. These were some of the drastic clearances necessitated by the building of the huge St John's Precinct. In the same period Queen Square with its fruit and vegetable market disappeared. For a short time I worked in this market and many people felt that its destruction was a sad end to a quaint old part of Liverpool. The bustling market with its colourful characters should have remained as part and parcel of everyday life of the city centre. Ironically it has since been declared that the square and its surrounding streets need not have been demolished at all. St John's Lane still stands as a thoroughfare but only one of its buildings avoided the bulldozer and has since been renovated. Lime Street, probably Liverpool's most famous street, did not escape the redevelopment of the 1960s. The view of St George's Hall from the north end of Lime Street in 1964 (see photo below) shows one of the huge Victorian blocks which was removed to make way for the St John's Precinct development. Lime Street took its name from the limekilns that stood there in the eighteenth century (the site of the present railway station). In recent years the street was one of Liverpool's most attractive by night, the neon lights helping to create its unique character. The character of the city centre in general is now much diminished compared with the 1960s and seems likely to decline further in the future.

Close to Lime Street stands Clayton Square where some of the structures are 200 years old. These buildings have been demolished to make way for new shops. The thought of the remains of this Liverpool square being destroyed is diabolical. The lessons from the recent past are obviously still being ignored with the continued sweeping away of what little is left of Liverpool's character. Queen Square no longer exists; Williamson Square is but a shadow of its former self and it appears Clayton Square is destined for a similar fate.

St Paul's Square, photographed in 1966 overshadowed by the John Moores Centre then under construction. Once the centre of Liverpool's Welsh community, the square took its name from St Paul's Church erected here in 1769.

The Greyhound pub, demolished in 1977, was at the corner of Tithebarn Street and Hatton Garden.

The Justice Hotel photographed in splendid isolation in desolate Marybone, just prior to demolition in 1981.

*Stockdale Street, off Marybone.
This terraced street was cleared in
the late 1960s and the new inner
ring road now runs across the
ground upon which it once stood.*

*Great Charlotte Street, one of a number
of old market streets destroyed during the
construction of the huge St John's Precinct.
In the foreground is the old pub
The Spanish House Hotel, at the junction with
Whitechapel. The Royal Court Theatre can
be seen in the background. Photographed in
1970, this section of Great Charlotte Street is
now a car park.*

*The Stork Hotel, Queen Square.
The hotel was a former town house,
older than the property surrounding
it and is shown during demolition
in 1976.*

Queen Square, off Great Charlotte Street, still had a fruit and vegetable market in the 1960s.

St John's Lane, named after a late 18th century church which once stood on the site of St John's Gardens behind St George's Hall. The hotel, The Victorianna, at the junction with Roe Street, was demolished in 1965.

Lime Street in 1964, showing St George's Hall. Beyond it stands one of the massive Victorian buildings which were later demolished to make way for St John's Precinct. St George's Hall was completed in 1854 and at the present time stands empty, (let's hope our city fathers never allow this magnificent Victorian structure to decay and become another building that's finally, as so many other examples in this book show, just came tumbling down).

Liverpool was founded as a borough in 1207, although ancient, no buildings have survived of ancient date, although a church has stood on the site of Our Lady and St Nicholas, Chapel Street since the 13th century (the oldest section remaining is a tower that was rebuilt in 1815, the rest of the church rebuilt after destruction during the war). The castle had all but gone by the 1720s, and the oldest surviving building is now the Bluecoat Chambers, originally built as a Charity School in 1717, whereas the Town Hall (the City's third) was built between 1749-1754.

It was from the 18th century, and particularly the 19th century that Liverpool expanded to eventually become the second City of the Empire. Surprisingly, the original 7 streets have survived, although greatly altered in width. They are: Chapel Street, Bank Street (Water Street) Whiteacre Street/Mill Street (Old Hall Street) Moor Street (Tithebarn Street) Juggler Street (High Street) Castle Street and Dale Street.

Enormous changes have occurred over the years in town, as it's referred to, even though it's only approximately 1 square mile. Mass destruction happened during the war of course, when the Luftwaffe bombed the City. Fortunately, the Pier Head survived and the three main buildings remained, and for years have been regarded as the "face" of Liverpool worldwide. They have been referred to lately as the "three graces" I don't know where that came from, or particularly think appropriate, but nowadays accepted. Individually they are the Mersey Dock and Harbour Building, 1907, now referred to as the Port of Liverpool Building, the Royal Liver Building, 1911, and the Cunard Building, 1916. A more comprehensive history of Liverpool is written in my previous book, "Liverpool Our City, Our Heritage".

Pier Head L3

Although always referred to as the Pier Head, it's official name is George's Pier Head, after a former dock it replaced, George's Dock, which opened in 1771, and finally closed in 1900.

This view is from the 1960s, with the renowned Royal Liver Building in the background, and features the old "back loader buses". A decade earlier it would have been mainly trams, and a decade later predominantly "Atlantean buses" (one man operated).

Major alterations have since left the Pier Head void of any buses, and the tradition of the last buses leaving the Pier Head at midnight to all parts of the City has now been confined to history, with the extension of the Leeds - Liverpool canal now running right through the Pier Head into the Albert Dock.

South Castle Street/South John Street area Ll

This view, from 1949, shows the devastation caused by the Lufwaffe's bombing from the Second World War, with the Cathedral, still under construction, as if in defiance in the background. Into the new millennium most of what remained after the bombing has been obliterated. The year 2008 brought about massive changes in this area, after Liverpool won the European Capital of Culture, with the new "Liverpool 1" shopping Mall having opened, also the Echo arena, and the BT Convention Centre on the dock estate, which has completely transformed the whole area.

South John Street L1

Just one of the numerous structures destroyed during the hostilities, a former pub, the Custom House Hotel, reduced to a shell after bombing in the 1940s.

Irwell Street L3

Named after the Mersey and Irwell navigation Act of 1720, which enabled barges to travel as far as Manchester. Formerly located off Mann Island, with the Albert Dock in the background when photographed in 1988, these early 19th century houses were demolished in the early 1990s. Then into the new millennium, a complete transformation, Mann Island was the site for the proposed "cloud", a controversial structure that was finally rejected, yet what was built. Two structures of black granite, and a new Museum are also controversial, love them or loathe them, they are now part of the landscape.

James Street/Strand Street L1

A rather drab structure at this junction when photographed in 2008, although the pub, displaying the name "Cooper's", was a very popular venue for pub-goers whilst it remained open. The block was finally demolished in 2010, and somewhat strangely this prime site is still awaiting development in 2013.

Goree Warehouses L2 and L1

With the modern trend to turn warehouses into apartments, what would this pile be worth today? The Goree Warehouses were originally built in 1780, and then rebuilt in 1802 after a disastrous fire. Although war damage did occur, they were crudely demolished in the 1950s. This resulted in a much wider Strand/ Goree, which in turn created the Pier Head to become somewhat isolated, particularly as traffic increased, even more so when the buses ceased terminating there. It was all change again when the new canal link was constructed into the Albert Dock.

Centre/left is Albion House, still standing, formerly named the White Star Building (1898) at the junction of the Strand and James Street.

Facing where the overhead railway fades out of view, stands another magnificent landmark the old Custom House, partly shown (1828-1839) another sad loss. Built on the site of the Old Dock, as with the latter damaged during the war, but quite repairable, but with no foresight whatsoever, demolished! How complimentary it would have been to the facing Albert Dock had it survived (see next view).

Canning Dock/Salthouse Dock/Albert Dock

These docks 'still working' when photographed in 1948, and the huge Custom House, Canning Place, yet to be demolished at the time, located facing the bridge between the Canning Dock and Salthouse Dock. Yet just over two decades later, these docks would become derelict, and by the early 1970s all the south docks became redundant, and lying derelict. In fact only after Michael Heseltine's intervention after the Toxteth riots in the early 1980s was the Albert Dock saved from demolition, the country's largest grade one structure, and massive tourist attraction, and is now completely transformed, with the Maritime Museum, apartments, bars, and restaurants, as well as Tate Liverpool.

Sadly, another structure shown on this view was not as lucky, the warehouses on Dukes Dock, shown in the centre, immediately south of the Albert Dock. The loss of this magnificent six storey warehouse was irreplaceable, its destruction in the 1960s was just simply civic vandalism at its worst. Older than the Albert Dock, it was opened in 1773 by the Duke of Bridgewater at the south end of Salthouse Dock as a distribution point and outer channel for his canal system to Runcorn. Goods were transported by "flats" and after 1800 it was named the Dukes Dock. The warehouses were built in 1811, apparently by French Napoleonic prisoners of war. Two large "caverns" can be clearly seen, which enabled the barges to pass through, and similar to the old Custom House, had it survived it would have been a wonderful complement to the Albert Dock.

Sailors Home L1

Sadly, more civil vandalism, this superb building, formerly in Canning Place, (1846-1852) then after a disastrous fire in 1860, rebuilt in 1862. The Home, a Seaman's Lodging House, had a courtyard and cast iron balconies reminiscent of the old sailing ships, but this superb building was demolished in the 1970s. Somewhat ironically, the former Gates of the Sailors Home were unveiled on the 19th August 2011 on Paradise Street close to the original site. (a separate view is on page 186).

"Gates"

The Gates, known as the Henry Pooley Gates, and listed, were taken down in 1951 for repairs, but ended up languishing outside a foundry in the Midlands, and after 60 years are finally back, due to a hard fought campaign by local man Gabriel Muies to bring them back home to Liverpool.

Flying Dutchman PH L1
This view c.1908, when the vicinity was inundated with pubs, located at the junction of Canning Place, and Litherland Alley and was part of a building named Revenue Chambers. It survived the devastation in the area during the war, but not the bulldozer, and was demolished in the 1970s, the site now part of the Liverpool 1 development. (a later view is on page 187).

Eagle PH L1
This pub, 81 Paradise Street was photographed in 1995, when still trading, although no longer a pub, the building, and the adjoining buildings still remain, albeit in completely different surroundings to former days. The thoroughfare is now part of the Liverpool 1 Shopping Mall and was previously located close to the Old Dock, thriving during the 18th, 19th and 20th centuries, and in fact together with Whitechapel, and Canning Place, was laid out over the original "Pool" that flowed into the river. This was before the Old Dock was constructed that changed the fortunes of Liverpool, as more and more docks were constructed.

Eagle PH
This is the pub in 2011, and not a great deal of difference externally from the earlier view, the plaque now on the premises states the following... (see next page).

Plaque

The strong connection with America was well illustrated here in the 19th century, as shown on the plaque (left and below).

Pre 1880s, this pub was actually named the American Eagle, and other 19th century pubs on Paradise Street with American named connections were 13, the Red White and Blue, 20/22 The American Shed, and 45 The American Saloon.

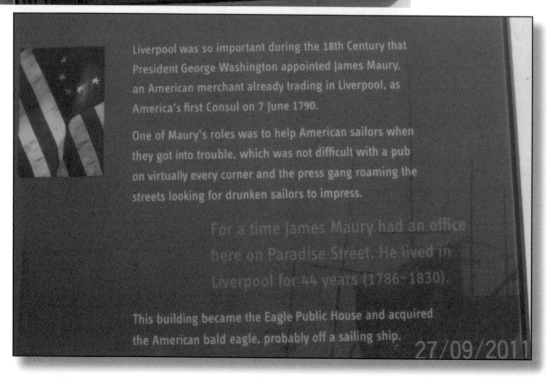

Hanover Street/Duke Street L1

The Casartelli Building at the corner of Duke Street and Hanover Street, despite being a listed building was senselessly pulled down; this view is from the 1970s, again, wanton civil vandalism. However in my opinion just as bad was the demolition of the adjoining and older warehouses on Hanover Street. The Casartelli Building was rebuilt, with the façade similar to the original, and the Echo's "stop the rot" campaign, still ongoing, uses the Casartelli Building as its logo.

Warehouses L1
Adjoining the Casartelli Building at 24/30 Hanover Street, shown in 2000, they were also listed, and have also been re-built on the old warehouse style, albeit now modern apartments.

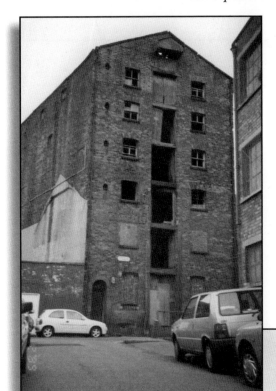

Argyle Street L1

A narrow street adjacent to Hanover Street, featuring a typical 19th century warehouse, once so common in the City Centre, and the north and south dock road areas. A number have been demolished over the years, but with the modern trend of conversion to apartments, many have since been converted, such as the one, shown here, photographed from Seddon Street in 1999, when still in a derelict state.

Brooks Alley Ll

This narrow alley, 91 yards long still remains, found between Hanover Street, and Old Post Office Place, with a few old warehouses still standing, including this view, which as shown, was last in use as a café. At the junction with Hanover Street in the early 20th century was a PH named the Lyceum, (featured in A Pub On Every Corner Volume 1) displayed on the wall was the original spelling of this alley, which in those days was Brooks's Alley.

Berry Street L1
A typical flamboyant Victorian PH, the Neptune, numbered 33/35 Berry Street, at the junction of Knight Street, photographed in the 1920s. Although it was still open in the early 1960s, it never survived the era.

Berry Street L1 - *The other corner of Knight Street, and two adjoining pubs, c.1904, the first was the Napier House, numbered 37, and the Masonic, number 39. Although this block was demolished long before the war, (not to be confused with another PH, the Masonic, numbered 21/23 Berry Street, which still remains, although having had various name changes).*

Grapes PH Ll - *This pub still remains, higher up Knight Street, albeit having been altered over the years from this view, c.1908, numbers 35 Knight Street and 60 Roscoe Street, so why included in this publication? The vicinity is completely different nowadays from the time of the previous photograph. Between Berry Street and Roscoe Street, a slum area existed alongside the more well-to-do houses nearby, such as Rodney Street, when the poor lived cheek by jowl with the more wealthy, and this view features a small reminder of what was once common throughout the City, a court entrance adjacent to a pub, shown on the extreme left.*

Upper Hope Place L7
Due to the irregular old boundaries of this vicinity, this is officially in Edge Hill, but for all intents and purposes classed as town, It stood off Hope Street. These fine old Georgian properties were demolished in the 1970s before such property was considered for renovation, although a small section still remains.

Mount Pleasant L3
This view is from 1964, all the old property on the right having since been demolished, including the Abercromby Vaults PH, numbered 130/132. The crane on the left was in use during the construction of the new Metropolitan Cathedral of Christ the King, which started in 1962, and opened in 1967. The wall was a remnant Livef what was once came biggest workhouse in the country, which had opened in 1842. The site was sold by the city council in 1930 for a proposed new Cathedral, which was intended to be one of the biggest in the world. However because of the expense, and the Second World War, it was never built (except for the crypt which still remains).

William Brown Street L3 - *This thoroughfare is now part of a "World Heritage Site", but not so when this photograph was taken in the 1890s, featuring the north side of the street, when the last of the old property was about to be obliterated, two pubs shown, the Leicester Hotel, and Angel Hotel, either side of Mill Lane, from a former total of 12 pubs, pre 1860s.*

Three magnificent structures were built here to compliment the nearby St George's Hall. The first was the Public Library and Museum, paid for by Merchant Banker, Sir William Brown, 1860, after whom the street was re-named shortly after completion, previously it was named Shaws Brow, (featured in Liverpool Our City, Our Heritage). The Walker Art Gallery, 1877, and the Picton Reading Room 1879, later the County Sessions House, 1884, and a Technical School, corner of Byrom Street, 1901 completed the north side of William Brown Street. (see next view).

William Brown Street L3 - *This view c.1904, with the new Technical School, bottom right, and partly showing the Library and Museum adjoining. The old block crossing the bottom of William Brown Street was on Old Haymarket, with the start of Dale Street looking west, (see Dale Street page 241) whereas the opposite corner is the junction of Dale Street and Byrom Street, looking north. All the property on Old Haymarket was demolished for the construction of the Mersey Tunnel (Queensway) which opened in 1934.*

William Brown Street L3 - *The Tunnel had been in use for nearly 30 years when this was photographed in 1962, the previous old property would have been fading from memory by then, yet another wave of demolition was to take place on this view some 30 years later. This time it was Manchester Street, shown on the left, which ran from Victoria Street to Dale Street, with all the property being demolished during the 1990s.*

Manchester Street L1

This view, photographed from Dale Street before the demolition started is from 1991 and features one of the well known "hostelry's" in Liverpool City Centre, Yates's Wine Lodge, number 12, one of the last to go from the traditional bare and basic "Winy's". Even today, arguments and conversations continue in pubs throughout the City as to how many existed in the City, so how many did exist?

The company was founded in Oldham in the 1880s, and the first wine lodge was actually in Dale Street, in the 1890s then one numbered 46 Great Charlotte Street, and 23 Deane Street, also in the 1890s (originally part of the same building, and before demolition of Deane Street they became separate premises) and the Great Charlotte Street Wine Lodge, now called the Blob Shop, is the last remaining of the old Wine Lodges. Before the First World War, three more appeared, 41 Moorfields, formerly a pub, the Cross Keys, 55 Lime Street, formerly a pub, the Horse Shoe, and 5 Manchester Street, formerly a pub, the Cumberland Hotel. By the 1930s, three more opened, also previous pubs, they were 23 Tarleton Street, formerly the Conway Castle, 7 Cases Street, formerly the Vine, and 12 Manchester Street, formerly the Oak Tree, a short lived one was also in the State Building, Dale Street (not the original). The Cumberland Hotel was demolished as part of the Mersey Tunnel scheme, so leaving 7 original Wine Lodges still trading after the last war, from a total of 9, the "modern" Wine Lodges, are not included in this list. Like all pubs they were frequented by regulars, well known for some crazy "characters" and a scroll was given out to the regulars, including myself, in this particular one as a joke, by regular John E Puddifer, which was the "WHINGEING WINOS CLUB" which caught on and grew in popularity, covering not just regulars, but many others who frequented the "Winy" from time to time (a list is printed in A Pub On Every Corner, *Volume 1). Sadly, many faithful customers are no longer with us.*

Manchester Street was opened in 1821 but, prior to that date coaches leaving Liverpool had to travel up Shaws Brow (later William Brown Street) the new route creating a much easier gradient. Yet since the demolition of the street, the name was also obliterated, now called Old Haymarket, which originally crossed the bottom of William Brown Street, see previous page.

Richmond Street/Williamson Square L1

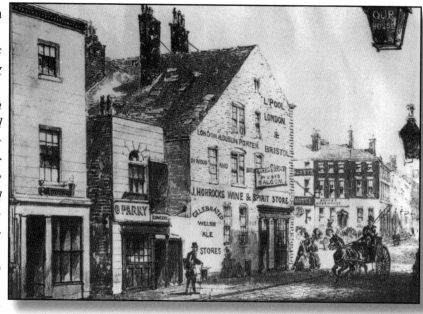

This drawing c.1859 is Richmond Street looking towards Williamson Square. The area was inundated with pubs at that period (described in detail in A Pub On Every Corner volume 1*) and four are on this view, the Concert Tavern, number 19 Richmond Street, displaying the manager's name as 0 Parry (Owen), the Queens Arms Music Hall, number 23 Richmond Street and 1 Williamson Square, also displaying the manager's name as J Horrocks (James) amongst other slogans, and the lamp of a pub in the forefront on Richmond Street, named Our House.*

On the eastern side of Williamson Square, partly shown, is the Star PH, adjoining a bonded warehouse, at the junction of Houghton Street, and by 1865 replaced by a new theatre named the Star Music Hall, which still had four separate drinking establishments, and also referred to as the Theatre Vaults during the 1870s. Then after reconstruction in 1911, it was re-named the Playhouse Theatre, home to the Liverpool Repertory Theatre Company. Major alterations then occurred in the 1960s, and the theatre remains to date (see page 234).

2011 - *The same view from 2011, with the Playhouse on the eastern side, the former Concert Tavern also still remains, albeit with various alterations, and possibly the next building, also with major alterations, whereas the predominant pub in the previous view, the Queens Arms Music Saloon at the time, also remains, and was still named the Queens Arms and trading as a pub into the new millennium. It was then converted into a bakery, and in 2009 converted into a betting shop.*

Queens Arms L1 - *The façade of the pub and adjoining building featured in this view when trading as a pub in the 1990s.*

Cases Street Ll

This view is looking towards the former Clayton Square from Ranelagh Street in the 1960s. Beyond the Midland Hotel are two more pubs still trading, the Globe Hotel and Coopers the sign indicating the name Coopers (formerly the Sefton Arms) is now at the end of this street, the rest demolished as part of the new Clayton Square shopping development. Just beyond Coopers a former pub Casey's Bar pre 1960s, was one of Yates's Wine Lodges.

Williamson Square Ll

The Williamson Square area was wiped out in the 1960s, sadly in the name of progress at the time, as the former narrow and quaint streets of the vicinity all vanished, and the redevelopment would become as so many other cities from this period. With hindsight the area would have no doubt been classed as some named "quarter" which is the trend today, but it wasn't to be of course, and the old block in the centre, yet to be demolished was Roe Street, with the centre building one of numerous pubs that were very popular in this area, the Magic Clock.

The top right was Queen Square, the old fruit and vegetable market, still bustling as trading continued amongst the demolition surrounding it, yet in no time this too would all be gone. The structure on the right, the Royal Court Theatre, Roe Street, is still standing, and viewing it now, it's hard to imagine what this part of town was like during the bustling 1960s.

Whitechapel Ll - *A former Higson's house, the Temple, photographed in 1956, formerly numbered 14/18, at the junction of Leigh Street. Shown on the right is Paradise Street, the continuation of Whitechapel, and now part of the new development of "Liverpool One".*

Adjoining the Temple, is the side elevation of the former flamboyant and well loved Bunney's department store, junction of Church Street. It was at this time that Greenwoods, the menswear chain took over Bunney's, and the building along with the pub were demolished to be replaced by a typical bland block of offices and shops that opened in 1959.

The same view from 2011
Photographed from the corner of Leigh Street, near the end of 2011, it was announced that the block itself would be demolished in 2012, for a flagship retail store, and with it a slice of Beatles history would be lost.

At the time of writing (in late 2012) the block has already been demolished, and a new structure under construction. Before demolition, a well-known Liverpool solicitor, Rex Makin, had an office here, and back in the 1960s, Brian Epstein was based here, working in the family business NEMS (North End Music Stores) and it was in this office that the Beatles signed the contract that would ultimately lead them to world domination in the music industry.

Victoria Street Ll

Patriotism in full bloom on the Liverpool Daily Post *and* Echo *Building, Victoria Street, for Queen Elizabeth II's Coronation in 1953. Michael James Whitty had founded the* Daily Post *in 1855 in a small printing shop at 29 Lord Street (more information on Mr Whitty is in* A Pub On Every Corner Volume 4*). Alexander Jeans, after serving as a manager on the* Daily Post *founded the evening paper — the* Liverpool Echo *in 1879, publishing together with the* Daily Post *at the new Victoria Street premises. They left the Victoria Street site for their current site in Old Hall Street in 1972, with the old site now Millennium House.*

Old Hall Street L3

Three views of Old Hall Street indicating the pace of new building since the millennium, the first view is from 2000, showing early property still standing from its industrial past. Railway sidings, and an earlier canal basin in existence here in the late 18th Century,

Second view

Just three years later, 2003, and new hotel already well underway. Fortunately, one of the old blocks has been preserved and incorporated into the new hotel. (partly shown behind the hoardings).

Third view

The conversion of the early houses, long established and saved as part of the hotel when photographed here in 2011.

Jackson Lane L3

Huge warehouses undergoing demolition in Jackson Lane and Queen Street, off the western side of Old Hall Street. These huge relics of the industrial past were photographed in 1969.

It was in this area that a 13th Century mansion house existed, occupied for over 400 years by the Moore family, who moved to Bankhall so the previous abode became the 'Old Hall' giving Old Hall Street its name. The site of Jackson Lane and the vicinity was built on in the early 1970s for the Royal Insurance Company, and the Liverpool Daily Post *and* Echo *buildings.*

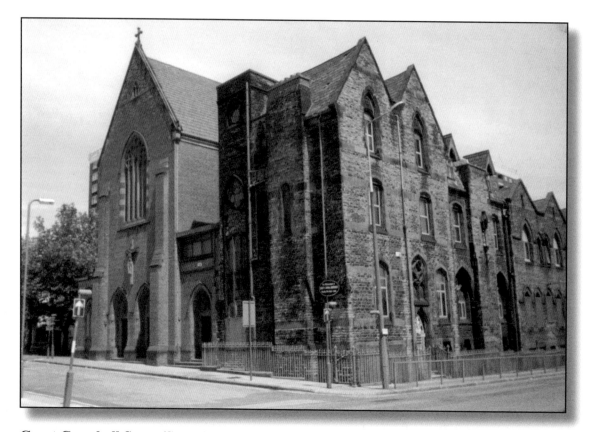

Great Crosshall Street/Standish Street L3

The Church of Holy Cross photographed in 2003. This was once a densely populated Catholic area, and some years ago the church would have been full with its regular congregation. Sadly, like so many other parish churches, as the population dwindled, and moved away, so making impossible the up-keep of the church, and this particular one was demolished within a couple of years.

Johnson Street L3
These three storey cellar houses would have been in the parish of Holy Cross when numerous similar houses existed in the densely packed area - photographed in the 1930s. Running from Dale Street to Marybone, the old houses now long vanished and this view was north towards Marybone shown at the top of the photograph, the more modern houses that replaced the older ones have also been cleared, and since the millennium student flats now proliferate in the area.

Dale Street L2

One of the original 7 streets, and the main route into/out of the town for centuries. Numerous inns and taverns once lined this thoroughfare, particularly during the 19th Century. One of the most notable was the Saracen's Head, located on the part of the land where the Municipal Building now stands. In its heyday, around 1830, some 30 coaches a day left/arrived at this inn before the railway gradually took over that mode of travel.

Throughout the 19th Century grand commercial buildings began to replace the old inns of Dale Street, particularly along the south side of the street, with many now enjoying listed status. Prior to the 1860s, the south side of Dale Street down to Whitechapel was a huge slum area and this was mainly cleared when a new thoroughfare was laid out, named Victoria Street. The only reminder of its past is the still remaining narrow alleys, a few still stand off the north side of Dale Street, such as Hackins Hey, which has a dated pub (1726), the Hole in the Wall, (described in *A Pub On Every Corner Volume 1*, and *Liverpool Our City Our Heritage*). The following are just two of the many former pubs of the area.

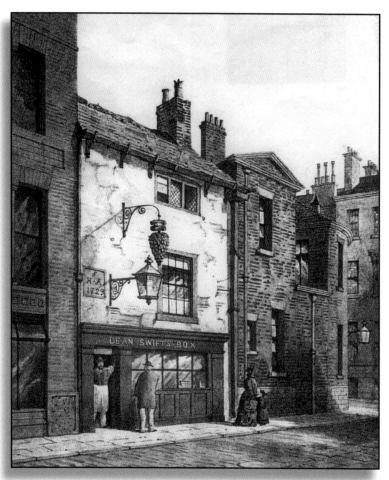

Dean Swift's Box L2

One would have thought that this early 18th century drawing showing an old pub dated 1729 would have tumbled down many years ago, yet the structures on this view still remain, albeit with major alterations. Over the years, but for this view, numerous people would have passed, and still pass this block never realising it was a former pub, or how old the structures are. It's located in an alley off the south side of Dale Street, Sweeting Street, named after Alderman, Sweeting, who was Mayor of Liverpool in 1698. The street would have been laid out shortly after his tenure, and was later named Elbow Lane, before changing back to Sweeting Street, and is located almost opposite to the previously mentioned Hackins Hey. This too had public houses like the "Hole in the Wall". The older parts of town became inundated with pubs throughout the 18th Century, many in alleys such as this, and by the 1820s five pubs were in Sweeting Street alone!

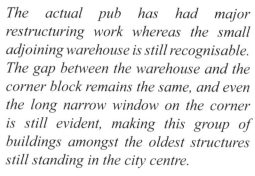

The actual pub has had major restructuring work whereas the small adjoining warehouse is still recognisable. The gap between the warehouse and the corner block remains the same, and even the long narrow window on the corner is still evident, making this group of buildings amongst the oldest structures still standing in the city centre.

06/04/2011

Dale Street/Old Haymarket L2
This was the last structure on the south side of Dale Street, a former pub named the Viaduct Vaults, (also shown on the early William Brown Street view page 230). Numbered 160 Dale Street and 37 Old Haymarket. Note the upper rooms, in use as a Restaurant, the Claret, when photographed in the 1890s, it was later named the Junction Vaults before demolition as part of the new Mersey Tunnel scheme.

Seymour Street L3
Both sides of this thoroughfare contained listed buildings, early brick built terraced houses, some dating from as early as 1810, and others the 1820s, but come the 1980s and this view of the west side shows the demolition of these fine Georgian houses.

The east side remains, well at least the façade, because similar to Shaw Street, they were completely ripped out, and turned internally into office space.

Fraser Place L3
An early 19th Century warehouse amongst a hotchpotch of early three storey houses still standing when photographed in 1989. It was only 26 yards in length, and was located off Fraser Street, which still stands between London Road and Islington, and is currently barren.

For decades Liverpool has suffered from having a negative image particularly from the south of the country, made worse by certain comedians who stereotyped all Scousers as 'Scallies' and the aftermath of the Hillsborough disaster in 1989 had the country as a whole (except in Merseyside) portraying 'Scouse hooligans' who caused the disaster.

As ever, the Scouse spirit prevailed and shortly before this publication was going to print, the truth was finally revealed after 23 years of perseverance that it was a huge cover up, with total vindication for Liverpool supporters. The implications are beyond this book, but thankfully the truth has finally come out, exonerating the fans from that fateful disaster.

The negative image of Liverpool was irradicated as the City of Culture year bought more and more people to the City, and since 2008 it has been classed as a vibrant place as visitors worldwide continue to visit the city.

However, the negativity was blatantly re-ignited into the second decade of the new millennium by a national newspaper (shades of the *Sun* newspaper?). The following comments are from *The Independent Newspaper* dated 29th February 2012, which in my opinion 'takes the biscuit' for knocking the Liverpool community.

The headlines are as follows
UN: BRITISH CITIES
HAVE 'NO-GO'
DRUGS ZONES

Three photographs then show a derelict view in Liverpool, Manchester and Birmingham (the Liverpool one featuring a derelict pub in Park Road Dingle, that has in fact been demolished).

Then the following under the photographs *"UN: drugs chief compares major British cities to worst areas of Brazil, Mexico and the United States claims 'law enforcement alone' cannot succeed police and MP reject Hamid Ghodse's assertions"*. (Professor Hamid Ghodse is President of the UN's International Narcotics Control Board: INCB).

Then inside the paper on page 4, are two photgraphs, underneath them is the following text: *"Drug gangs have turned parts of the UK into 'no-go' areas warns UN expert"*

And the two photographs *"Rockfield Road in Anfield, Liverpool left and the Cidae de Deus shanty town in Rio De Janerio, right"*.

Along with all major British cities, the three mentioned do have drug problems, but this article is ridiculous, in fact complete and utter nonsense to compare Rockfeld Road with a shanty town in South America.

I will now record a section of the article that follows after the two photographs (shown on the next page):

"Britain has vastly lower violent crime rates than in Latin America or the United States. In Mexico, drug wars between rival cartels in 2010 accounted for the lives of 15,273 people. In Brazil the homicide rate – much of it linked to drugs – is around 50,000 murders a year. According to the British crime survey; Greater Manchester police dealt with 32 murders last year, Merseyside 23 and the West Midlands 74".

Independant Newspaper Wednesday 29/02/2012 (source)

Acknowledgements (alphabetical order)

John Arrowsmith

Howey Burns

Jimmy Campion

Ronnie Challinor

Michael Davies

Kay Donnelly

Frank Dugan

George Kelly

Maureen Kirby

Michael Mainwaring

Karl Maloney

Suzanne Lau

Alex Marr

Frank Paine

Paul and Colin Prior

Tommy Prior

Khristina Rainford

Phil Sarto

Jim Sheldrick

Carl and Eddie Stephens

Dominic Whelan

Fred Williams

Billy Whinnett

Liverpool Daily Post & Echo

Liverpool City Engineer's Deptartment

The staff at Countyvise Ltd, Birkenhead